Living Stress Free

Living Stress Free

Dr Bonnie Etta

Living Stress Free by Dr Bonnie Etta

This book is written to provide information and motivation to readers. Its purpose is not to render any type of psychological, legal, or professional advice of any kind. The content is the sole opinion and expression of the author, and not necessarily that of the publisher. Copyright © 2018 by Dr Bonnie Etta. All rights reserved. No part of this book may be reproduced, transmitted, or distributed in any form by any means, including, but not limited to, recording, photocopying, or taking screenshots of parts of the book, without prior written permission from the author or the publisher.

Brief quotations for noncommercial purposes, such as book reviews, permitted by Fair Use of the U.S. Copyright Law, are allowed without written permissions, as long as such quotations do not cause damage to the book's commercial value.

For permissions, write to the publisher, whose address is stated below.
Printed in the United States of America.

ISBN   978-1-949746-16-7 (Paperback)
ISBN   978-1-949746-17-4 (Digital)

Lettra Press books may be ordered through booksellers or by contacting:
Lettra Press LLC
1 303 586 1431 | info@lettrapress.com
18229 E 52nd Ave.
Denver City, CO 80249
www.lettrapress.com

CONTENTS

Dedication vii
Introduction ix

Chapter 1   Healing Love 1
Chapter 2   Preciousness of Forgiveness 15
Chapter 3   Simple Truth 25
Chapter 4   The Miracles Unity 41
Chapter 5   The Grace Of Appreciation 49
Chapter 6   Speak To My Heart 55
Chapter 7   The Force Of Faith 65

Part Two
Reign In Life

Chapter 1   Breaking Satanic Ties 87
Chapter 2   Walking In Your Blessing 99
Chapter 3   Effective Spiritual Warfare For Your Inheritance ... 113
Chapter 4   Strategic Prayers 123
Chapter 5   The Anointing For Successful Living 133
Chapter 6   A New Season 145
Chapter 7   Productive Faith 153
Chapter 8   Greater Grace 163
Chapter 9   Vision And Purpose 171

Notes And References 181
About The Author 189
About the Book 191

DEDICATION

I dedicate this book to you who desire true harmony and a song in the night.

Dr Bonnie Etta

INTRODUCTION

Stress, does it have a cure? Can I ever live stress free? Everywhere I go as I travel to the nations of the world teaching and counseling; I come in contact daily with people whose greatest illness is not HIV/AIDS or cancer nor any other terminal disease but whose greatest problem has to do with stress. Stress is one of the greatest cause for sickness and death in many parts of our world today. Stress is one of the main causes of the alarming rate of divorce and crime in the 'civilized nations'. Many people are suffering from the effects of stress directly or indirectly today than in any other time in history.

In a world with unusual political and economic instability and uncertainty, it seems as if the rich are victims of stress more than the poor. There appear to be more happy poor people than the rich counterparts. As I travel through continents like Africa, etc; I see very poor people but with smiling and happy faces every where I go. I see them sing and dance and celebrating life; with few things to worry about. Riches and wealth can never provide solution to the social and moral depravity and the stress problem in our world today.

Stress is a condition that must be dealt with wisely and intelligently by the help of the Holy Spirit. The Holy Spirit is called the Comforter; His presence is true liberty. His fruit is love, joy and peace. His power is the yoke destroyer. Your happiness does not depend on God; it depends on you. Your happiness depends on your attitude and response to the daily occurrences of your life. The way you respond to the situations of your life will determine how you will live your life; stress up and worn out or stress free.

This book is written to provide guidelines on how to deal with stressful situations wisely and intelligently, in order to make the best of every situation. With all my heart I wish you a happy and stress free life while we walk through the seasons of our earthly life. If you have no room for peace, you have made enough room for stress and pain. You were born to live a pleasant life and God has given us some recommendations that can guarantee absolute peace, love and joy in abundance. May you find help and healing as you read this timely book. Be stress free so you can help others live stress free lives through the power of the love of Jesus Christ.

Agbor B. Etta PhD

CHAPTER ONE

Healing Love

Love is like a mustard seed,
Planted by God and watered by men.

Muda Saint Michael

CHAPTER ONE
Healing Love

Love is the greatest healing force. Love heals, Halleluiah; love gives life. "In this was manifested the love of God towards us, because that God sent his only begotten Son into the world, that we might live through him", John 4:9.

Your love is your life; when you love you live; when you hate you die. The life of love is a wise choice, I counsel you to choose love and live. There is no profit in anger and resentment. There is no gain in jealousy and fighting. There is no profit in hatred.

Love is profitable to all; it is your health and your source of soundness and wellbeing. You need to discover the power of the love of God: Love begins with God. Love comes from God, for God is love and He loves you much more than you could ever imagine. The Apostle Paul spoke of the mystery of the love of God, Col 2:2.

God is love. God's love is so deep that we can never go under it; it is so wide that we can never go around it; it is so high that we can never go above it. God's love is not only for good people, for He gives the rain, the sun and free air to all. His heart of love extends his goodness to all, for his nature is love. Don't expect everyone to be kind and good to you, for not everybody has received the revelation of the love of God yet. Don't expect people to be perfect and right all the time, for no one is perfect; man will always have shortcomings and disappointments. Put your trust in the unchanging, ever perfect and unconditional love of God. Just keep on in your love lifestyle, for to love is more profitable than to hate. Continually choose love, for love is of God. Keep your heart healthy by being filled with the love of God.

The love for God is a wise response to the love of God. When someone you love gives you a present, you respond by accepting and receiving the gift; the way to respond to the love of God is by your love for God. Love responds to love. Your complete freedom from all the things that bring stress and tension in you is by responding to the love of God for your life and by loving God with all your heart. Your love for God is the power that suppresses and destroys all the forces that seek to distress and tear you apart.

Your love for God is the secret of a stress free life. The love for God has to do with: accepting the counsel of the Lord through his written and spoken word; accepting the way of the Lord rather than your own way. It has to do with your obedience and willful submission to the will of God. Love for God has to do with spending time with him in personal prayers, reading and studying his Precious Word.

Love God with all your heart for He loves you with all his being before the foundation of the world. When you manifest your love for God, you cause Him to pay greater attention to you and to all that concerns you, for He cares for you especially because you are intimately connected to Him. Step out for God and all the host of heaven will step forth for you. Stand up for God and the Holy Spirit will go on with you.

Just love the Lord no matter what happens.
When people hate you, love the Lord.
When they love you, love the Lord.
When people hurt you, love the Lord.
When they appreciate you, love the Lord.
When people gossip and give false report about you, love the Lord.
When they accept and approve of you, love the Lord.
When people plan evil against you, love the Lord.
When they cooperate with you, love the Lord.

When people fight against you, love the Lord.
When they support you, love the Lord.
When in tribulations love the Lord.
When in celebration, love the Lord.
When you go through loses because of your faith, love the Lord.
When you pickup a better job, love the Lord.
Love the Lord in prosperity and in adversity.
In all that you do, let the love of God direct and guide you through life. Just love God no matter what.

Love your brother and sister, love your neighbors and colleagues because you love God and you are loved by God. The love of God in you is revealed in loving others. Love cannot be concealed it has to be expressed. Extend the love of God in you to other people. You are loved to love; you are alive to give life. You are saved to save others through the love of God.

"For God so love the world, that he gave his only begotten Son, that whosoever believes in him should not perish but should have everlasting life", John 3:16.

You will live much longer if you fill your heart with love for others. Refuse to be pulled into the pain of hatred, stress and tension by the limitations and weaknesses of others. You should ignore the ignorance of others and move forward with peace and calm in your heart. Always remember that there is more profit in love than in hate and quarrelling.

Let your love for others gradually affect your immediate community. As you love, you become a channel of blessing and life. As you choose to love, you choose to put a smile on the faces of others.

Let your love lifestyle affect people and transform your community positively. Heal yourself and your community through the love revolution. You were not born to be killed by stress. Handle everything that may come your way with a smile. Surround your heart with love; let nothing break the walls of love around your heart, for in love is your health and in love is your life. If you love life, love one another. Love yourself, because God loves you. Love yourself because you love God.

Love yourself because you love others and because you love your community. Seek for ways to improve the state and condition of your community for good. Because you love God and you love yourself, you need to take good care of yourself. Separate from all that causes pain and offenses. Stay apart from all forms of disorder and conflicts.

Protect yourself from wrong influence and wrong habits. Keep your heart clean and your mind healthy. Keep yourself under the mighty hand of God, and stay away from ungodly practices. Because you love yourself, you should value your life more than your wealth. You should value your life more than your job. Value your life more than your business engagements. Value your life more than your appointments. Don't die for money, don't die for your job and don't cause yourself to die before your rightful time because of your overloaded schedule. Love yourself. Make time for just yourself, make time for enough sleep. Take time to rest and relax. Make time to enjoy good food; take time to play and to exercise yourself. The value of your life should come before that of your business and achievements. Put your life first, before seeking for wealth.

Don't pursue things at the expense of your life. Remember you are more valuable than all the wealth you can ever possibly possess. God loves you; you have no life without loving God. God loves you; you have an assignment to love others. Because God loves you, you have to love yourself and love others as God loves you. Love is a secret to stress free life. True love never fails, so just keep on loving.

Seven reasons why many refuse to walk in love

Deep Hurt

I grew up as a teenager hating my father, and wished him dead. In the depths of my heart I did not want to see him. I cannot forget what really happened. My mother was really sick and was in bed all day; my father walked in and saw my mom lying in bed. He did not care for my mother's health condition; instead he asked for his food and when it was not served as usual, he went to the bed where my mom was lying and started punching and kicking her all over her body. I tried to pull him and to defend my mom from the blows but my father pushed me out of the way and continued punching my desperate mother. I heard my mom crying and wishing God will take her life.

From that day I erased my father from my heart, and put an X on him. I saw him as a wicked man who did not care and as a result of all these I hated him. I refused to love him as my Dad.

There are some of you who think you have genuine reasons to hate or to refuse to walk in love. Your reasons may be very convincing and your story may be very pathetic; but in all, when we stand before the Lord, He will tell you, "my child, I loved you while you were still messed up; I loved you while you were still a sinner".

He will tell you, "you can never change any person through hatred; but rather you change people by loving them. You change people by showing them concern".

I decided to take my father as a prayer project, rather than hating I began to take him to God in prayers. I forgave him and submitted to him in love and reverence. When I felt hatred for my father, I was deeply sick within; I murmured against him and became stubborn in my heart. I came to realize that there was no profit in hating. When I decided to love him and to pray for his change, I was healed in my heart; I gained my personal peace of mind. Choose love; choose life, for love is life.

Unbelievable Discovery, Mistrust

A friend was traveling for a month vacation, this was in Africa where most people don't have bank accounts, she took her business money worth $400 and gave to her best friend to keep and this was what she said to her friend: "please I will be back in one month. I will need the money immediately I return; I could not leave the money in my house because of insecurity. See you soon". After one month the sister came to her friend for her money, but her friend told her to come after one week; after one week her friend could not produce the money. She had used the money, what a shame. Many old friends have become new enemies because of disappointments. I have been greatly disappointed by so many 'Christians'; there is a tendency to separate from friends who have shown great irresponsibility and lack of integrity.

You might say, "I can not continue with a friend who can not be trusted". That is true; but the Lord would say, "Ask of Me for wisdom to change and to transform and to influence your friend positively". You would get a testimony of a transformed friend. You might be the very one to help him or her out. Who knows, the weaknesses of your friend were made manifest to you, not for you to run away but for you to stand with him or her to help bring the needed change by the grace of God. By the grace of God you can still love even though disappointed.

Many marriages are breaking just because of mistrust; the 'unbelievable discovery'; the wife discovers that she was being cheated by the husband, or the husband discovered that the wife was not truthful at all. I am writing these pages today in the city of Venaria, Torino, Italy and I hear the Lord saying to you, "you can still make it; there is still a beautiful future for you". In Christ Jesus there will always be a way out if you wait upon the Lord patiently.

The Lord is able to help you go through the trying moments of your life; have a positive attitude, refuse to give in to pain; rather submit to the Holy Spirit. Hold your peace and control your mouth and actions.

I speak to you in the name of the Lord Jesus Christ our good example. Do not allow the weaknesses of people to rob you of your peace. Don't allow the unfaithfulness of other people make you unfaithful in any way. You are called to help the weak out of their weaknesses and to help out the unfaithful and the desperate. You can be the bridge of hope for a dying friend who needs just you to help him or her clean up and straighten up. Be available for a friend in need.

Pain

I can hear someone saying; "I am going through all this pain because of ..." Many nations are in pain because of their wicked political leaders who have no heart for their countrymen. There is nothing as frustrating and devastating as bad political regimes. They have no concern for the lives and development of their communities. Many Nations in Africa are crying because the future of their nations is ruined; everything has been sold out.

Youths are crying for lack of jobs, hospitals are crying for lack of equipment, while schools cry for lack of teachers; teachers are crying for lack of salaries. That person whom you think is the reason why you are going through your present crisis and situation, that person that has caused so much pain in your heart; it is time to release that person from your heart. I see a woman who is in tears because of the wickedness of her husband. You have been used and abandoned. You don't know how and what to do with your children.

Please, I would advice you to hand over the cause and source of your pains to God. Allow God to fight for you. He will give you the wisdom for the actions necessary. Don't act carnally or sensually. If you have to cry, cry out to God for He cares for you. His heart's desire is to wipe all tears from your eyes. The Lord knows your pain and will bring deliverance, for God is a very present help in times of need.

This is the time to lift up your eyes from your pain and from the cause of the pain. Turn yourself to the Lord and cry out to Him. When no one seems to understand you, God understands. When no one desires to listen to you, your God has all the time to listen, for he says: "Come and let us reason together" (Isa 1:18).

When no one has anytime to help you, Jesus would say to you: "For this reason I came to the earth and for this reason I died on the cross, for this reason I sent the Holy Spirit to be with you always and to be there whenever you need divine assistance".

I can hear him saying, "I will never leave you nor forsake you until I have performed that good thing and until I fulfill the yearning of your heart". Child of God, wipe your tears, for your pain will soon become a testimony.

Human Failures

Yesterday when I arrived in Rome, Italy, I could not see my luggage; when I was checking in my two bags I emphasized at the counter that I didn't want anything to happen to my bags and they reassured me that all would be well. You see, the airline failed me, I had to go with one attire for two days; it's a very unpleasant and undesirable experience.

You know, this is part of life; we have to face the unexpected and sometimes the unwanted. We live in a world full of failures and limitations; as long as you live people will fail you. Business partners will disappoint you when you need them the most. Be wise, be gentle, be careful and be intelligent. Understand the world in which you live. Lean on no one else except the Lord Jesus Christ.

Young lady; you have been deceived by several boy friends. Some even promised you unfathomable wedding just to go to bed with you and at the end you have been used, abused, and abandoned; and today you feel shattered, filled with hate and confused.

I do greatly empathize with you, the end has not come yet; clean up yourself, be wise and cling unto Jesus the Lord, the faithful and the infallible God. He has another beginning for your life and the future is far and much better than the past. Don't destroy your future because of your past encounters. Bury your past and dream a new dream for your life. Just learn to take a new step of faith, trusting Jesus Christ to lead each step of the way.

Let the pain of your past create in you a determination for a better and joyful future through Christ Jesus. My dear friend, gain wisdom from God for happy living; the lack of Godly wisdom has led many to painful and awful ends. Jesus doesn't want to see you cry any more; His will is your happiness, He wants to see you smile. I want to see you smile.

Deal with people with faith in God; deal with people with caution and discernment, never you trust a 'stranger'. Listen to the voice inside you.

Live life with eyes and ears wide open; don't die because of foolishness and carelessness. Don't end up like Samson, mighty but blind and in captivity. Never share your secrets with 'Delilah'.

Childhood Abuse

Some years ago I met a young lady who said these words to me. "I can never forgive my father for what he did to me, he raped me several times, and he divorced my mother and turned me into his sexual partner while I was still thirteen. I had to run away from home just to save my life, can you imagine? My father would promise me everything just to have sex with me. It was terrible".

What do you do with people that the evil one had used to abuse and to desecrate your life? What do you tell a victim of sexual abuse?

I can never forget an encounter with a young girl, who was raped by four men by the roadside; she ended up pregnant and with HIV/AIDS. It is very painful and stressful; something too bad to wish for anybody. Because of the pregnancy she was dismissed from school and she was driven from home by her parents who refused to sponsor her maternity needs. She had to come to my office for assistance. It is very painful to understand what this innocent girl went through at the age of fourteen.

Permit me to address you personally, I can feel your heart beats right now; the undesirable fresh memories of that past awful incident are flashing through your mind right at this moment that is why I am here to let you know that Jesus heals broken minds and hearts and completely mends broken lives. He did it for me he can do it for you. Open up and tell it all to Jesus Christ in simple prayer.

You have been praying to forget and to wipe it out of your mind but have not been able; there is still hope in the Lord Jesus.

Say this aloud:
Lord, I forgive from my heart. I forgive all of them in the name of Jesus Christ, halleluiah.

Please dear reader, let go of the past; the past is past and it's dead; bury it and move forward. Stand in faith in the power of the Word of God. Your God will heal and restore your life as you begin to take hold of every promise of God. Tell the enemy nothing will destroy your God given vision. Decide to love even those whom the devil used as tools against your life. What the devil meant for evil, your God will turn it out for good, praise God.

Rejection

"He came to his own but his own received him not" Jn 1:10.

You may be one of the millions who have suffered because someone you looked up to, refused to give you the love and attention you deserved in that time of need. These are the words of a fourteen–year–old West African teenager; "My father refused to send me to school because I am a girl; he said to me that he would keep his money to send the boys to school; he said he preferred to give me to marriage than to waste his money to sponsor me', Tiko, 2006.

Some are rejected because of their gender, others because of their tribe or nationality; some are rejected due to their social status. Never forget that the person you refused to help today might be the one to help you some day. The "Mandela" you sent to prison today might be your president tomorrow. The Joseph you mistreat today might be the one to sustain your life tomorrow.

My dear friend, if you have no one to identify with, Jesus is 'the' someone very special to identify with. If there is no one to embrace you, Jesus is ever ready with arms wide open for you. There is a place for you in Christ. There is a place for you in the house of God and there is a place for you in heaven, as long as you embrace Jesus as your Lord and Savior, Halleluiah.

If no one values or has regard for your person, Jesus calls you His own, His chosen, precious and well beloved. You have someone who is for you; his name is Jesus Christ the only Son of God. You are never alone.

Shattered Dreams

Many refuse to love because of hopelessness and desperateness; consequently, they develop anger and envy against any successful person that comes their way. They blame others for not showing them the love and concern they expect to receive and as a result they become furious and aggressive.

The good news is that Jesus is specialized in rebuilding broken lives and he is able to rebuild your shattered dreams. God has a divine and a unique reason for your existence. Believe him for a new beginning. He is able to put all things together again. Love heals; refuse to put the blame on others. Reject anger and envy, refuse to walk in bitterness. Choose love and live, for God is love. Make that decision now, just love no matter what and take godly steps towards the rebuilding of your life.

CHAPTER TWO

Preciousness of Forgiveness

"You will know that forgiveness has begun when you recall those who hurt you and feel the power to wish them well."

CHAPTER TWO
Preciousness of Forgiveness

Forgiveness is precious and forgiveness is of God. God's kindness towards us is manifested in our forgiveness. He forgives us because he loves us. Forgiveness is possible. You can be forgiven and you can forgive from the depth of your heart. Real forgiveness brings inner freedom and peace. When you refuse to forgive, you put yourself in a very unpleasant situation. You become a prisoner of your own conscience; you hurt your emotions and eventually, you lose your peace of mind. It is more advantageous to forgive than to die with pain in your soul.

Forgiveness brings freedom from acute and accumulated stress; forgiveness heals your weary heart. Forgiveness brings light in a dark heart. Forgiveness brings goodness in an offended and bitter heart. It will take forgiveness to put a smile in a wounded heart. Many are dying of cancer due to refusal to forgive and bitterness in the soul; either they refuse to be forgiven or they refuse to forgive.

Choose to forgive; do not harbor people or hurts in your heart any more. Your precious heart was not made for that. Take away all excess baggage from your heart. Learn to forgive for your life's sake. Forgiveness will prolong your years and un-forgiveness will shorten your days on earth. Be wise. Forgiveness has to do with the grace to let go. Forget what happened; take it from your heart. Stop focusing your mind on the painful memories of past incidents. Whatever happened, happened for a specific reason which you will come to understand with time.

Let go of the man who engaged you and dumped you just months to your planned wedding day.

Let go that person who has spread false stories about your life, just to destroy your personality and reputation because of jealousy.

Let go for God understands and He will surely avenge for you in due time; don't take judgment into your hands. Let go that individual that has caused you much failure in your life and business. Binding yourself to your past can never be of any good to you. Let it go and receive your peace; set your heart free.

Forgiveness has to do with denouncing all the offences and grievances; as well as all that was done against you or your family. It also has to do with all that has offended your heart and caused severe disorder in your whole system. It's time to look beyond your pains and the people the enemy used as instrument of grieve.

Forgiveness has to do with you casting behind you all that your enemies thought against you and their failed evil intensions.

Refuse to dwell on them, refuse to entertain them, refuse to allow your precious heart to be influenced and mastered by offences and crisis. You can be stress free.

Forgiveness releases your true beauty, the beauty of a peaceful character. It is more blessed to be simple and happy than to be sophisticated, unhappy, stressed–up, and worn out and offended with life. You need to forgive yourself; you are not an Angel. As long as you still have flesh and blood it is certain that you are bound to make mistakes in life; forgive yourself for the shortcomings of your life. Don't allow your failures to destroy your faith in God and faith for your future.

Don't destroy yourself because of your limitations; rather be challenged to do better in Jesus name. You were not born by God to be stressed up; His will is for you to smile out. Be filled with beauty and glory. True forgiveness has to do with true repentance. God does not forgive sins because they are confessed; he forgives sin because they are repented of. Confession without true repentance is just dead religion and ineffective.

True repentance brings true forgiveness. Some people find it hard to say, 'I am sorry'; they find it hard to realize their wrong; they see themselves too big to ask for forgiveness. You know what? You are just preserving yourself for more difficult days, for it takes true forgiveness to gain access to heaven. All glory to our God.

For your peace sake do forgive them and release them from your heart. Hand them over to God and refuse to hate them. Make a difference by forgiving them. Don't allow them to convert you to their side; unforgiving kills, forgiveness gives health and a sound heart. Decide to be a person who forgives.

Be a Joseph for he was a forgiver; he forgave his brothers of all the evil and pain they caused him to go through. These are the words of Joseph: "But as for you, ye thought evil against me; but God meant it unto good, to bring to pass, as it is this day, to save much people alive. Now therefore fear you not: I will nourish you, and your little ones. And he comforted them and spake kindly unto them". Gen 50:20-21.

Please decide to forgive; do what Joseph did; just forgive and become a blessing to all those who meant evil for you.

Decide to release pain from your heart through forgiveness. King David had to release his son Absalom from his heart.

Remember all that Absalom did to his father, King David; he killed his brother Amnon, David's first born son. Absalom sought to kill his father King David to take over his throne. Absalom had to lie sexually with his father's concubines openly to prove that he had no respect for his father anymore.

King David after some years had to decide to release Absalom from his heart and to forgive him, that was the right decision. I plead on you my dear reader to prayerfully release that person from your heart. It may be your parents, your husband or wife, your pastor or a colleague. Whoever it may be, please forgive and set your heart free, praise God.

Decide to gain total victory over all that the enemy sent against your life to cast you down emotionally, morally and spiritually.

Gain control over your past and present circumstances. Don't allow problems to control you. Take charge of the trying moments of your life and stand by faith in the power of the Word of God. Just do all that the Word says you should do and you will get the result that the Word promised you would get. Halleluiah!

Decide to keep your heart clean, sound and lively. Decide to secure your heart from words that are sent to crush you down. Reject every evil spoken word against your life and future.

Meditate on the words of Jesus Christ in the New Testament.

Meditate on the love of God demonstrated through Jesus Christ.

Meditate on the grace and mercy of God revealed through the cross of Jesus Christ.

Meditate on the faithfulness and goodness of God.

Meditate on the reward of peace and true harmony.

Refuse to defile your precious heart with the passing pleasures of this world. Don't give the enemy any room in your heart; keep your heart safe and clean, far from the reach of the devil. Refuse satanic inspired ideas.

Refuse thoughts of backsliding and thoughts of frustration. Have control of your heart, keep your heart with all diligence; keep it clean. Praise God!

You can do it in the name of Jesus Christ

Decide to have a forgiving and forbearing spirit; there is no sin that God cannot forgive; He will give you the grace to forgive all who sin against you. As long as you are alive be sure that offenses will come.

Be ready to forgive the offender and to cast the offenses behind your back and move forward in Jesus name. When you choose to forgive, you choose to live a happy life. When you refuse to forgive, you refuse yourself the privilege of a peaceful and a satisfied life. I choose to be a forgiver. Forgiveness will bring new life and healing to your stressed and wounded heart.

Choose to forgive

Cain killed his brother Abel because of bitterness and jealousy.

The sons of Jacob killed the men of Shechem because of great bitterness; because the prince of Shechem raped Dinah their sister. They made up their minds to eliminate the city of Shechem because they had no place for forgiveness in their hearts.

Unforgiving kills. When you refuse to forgive, you willingly set your heart on fire for evil and you unconsciously prepare your heart as a nursery for evil thoughts to grow on.

Joseph was so much blessed by God because he had a forgiving heart. His brothers were so afraid that Joseph would somehow revenge the evil they did to him; but Joseph had a clean and forgiving heart. He let go the painful past and embraced his brothers with love and goodness. Let's forget the pains of the past bitter experiences of our lives; forgive for your life's sake and for love's sake.

King David had to forgive his exiled son Absalom; who had killed his brother Amnon. (2 Sam 13:28).

But Absalom did not forgive his father the king. He seduced the entire nation of Israel for a civil war to kill his father in order for him to be king instead of his father. He ended up dying in battle. 2 Sam 19:10.

Judas who betrayed his master refused to forgive himself; even though Jesus had forgiven all offenses on the cross before his death: remember the prayer of Jesus on the cross; "Father forgive them". Judas went ahead to hang himself because he refused to forgive himself.

There is no profit in bitterness. Hardness of heart leads to self destruction and self affliction. I want to encourage you today to seek the Lord for the grace to forgive and to let go of all the pain others have caused you. That is part of life, you learn daily from the various encounters with various people. Your future is so precious; do not allow negative feelings to destroy you emotionally and psychologically.

Gain wisdom, the enemy is assigned to stress you in and out in order to draw you far from God and far from the life God intended for you; the goal and desire of the enemy is to ruin you and to destroy your soul. You must cast him out and shut the door to all forms of evil ideas and voices that suggest and impress upon your heart to revenge and to strike back. This is not to your advantage; this will result in adding salt to the wound. Seek solutions, seek peace, seek reconciliation, and seek to heal the hearts and minds of people. Begin by healing yourself and then reach out to others in Jesus name.

Call that friend of yours today and tell him or her; I have forgiven you in the name of the Lord Jesus Christ. God will be pleased with you and you will be pleased with the result. Forgiveness turns long time enemies to lifetime friends. When God forgave us, He turned us who were dead in sin into his well beloved sons and daughters.

Remember Esau the brother of Jacob vowed to see Jacob dead because he 'stole his birthright'. Because of the fear of Esau Jacob had to be a refugee far from home for more than twenty years. Jacob could not even be present at his mother's funeral and because of the fear of death it took him twenty long years to finally take the bold step to go back home trusting God for intervention. The Bible says that when Esau saw Jacob he ran and embraced him and kissed him peacefully. Because of forgiveness long term enemies became lifetime friends, halleluiah.

Forgiveness transforms angry people to loving and gentle individuals.

Forgiveness gives people the opportunity and the privilege to correct the mistakes of the past.

Forgiveness brings hope and grace to self condemned individuals.

Forgiveness gives assurance of true friendship.

Forgiveness is the manifestation of kindness and mercy.

Forgiveness is possible. Let us forgive one another as we have received the forgiveness of our sins from our Father above.

Your Temper

When people lose their temper, it does not stay in just the place where they lost it, but it travels miles away. And when they find and bind it, it may be, the act has been done, a mischief never to be healed, unto the farthest sun.

When people lose their temper it runs and rages far. It strikes at friends as well as foes, not caring who they are. And when it's cruel, force is spent. Its words and deeds go on down many ways through many days, un-reckoned and unknown.

When people lose their temper it never stays that way, its owner always finds it to use another day.

My Temper

When I lose my temper, I have lost my reasoning too. I am never proud of anything, which I angrily do. When ever I talk in anger and my cheeks become flaming red, I always utter something, which I latter would regret for saying it. In anger I have never done a kind or wise deed. I can't recall a single time when fury ever paid.

So I ask God for patience, for I've reached a wise age. I do not want to do a thing or speak a word in rage.

I have learned through sad experiences that when my temper flares, I never do a worthy, decent, or wise deed. Therefore I bring myself under subjection. I crucify my flesh and I submit to the power of the Holy Spirit; for without Him I can do nothing as I ought to do".

Evan Ken Krivohlavek

CHAPTER THREE

Simple Truth

"Unless your heart, your soul, and your whole being are behind every decision you make, the words from your mouth will be empty, and each action will be meaningless. Truth and confidence are the roots of happiness."

Unknown

CHAPTER THREE
Simple Truth

Truth, why truth? Truth is freedom, truth heals, truth is being real; truth liberates and sets free indeed. When you choose to walk in truth, you walk with personal inner freedom and self confidence; nothing to be ashamed of and nothing to hide. Truth is light, truth is being you. Truth is fearlessness and godliness. The moment you begin to allow the Spirit of truth to rule your life, you enter into a life of inner peace and boldness.

Where there is truth there is an assured future.

Where there is truth there is hope for healing, improvement and development.

Where there is truth there is hope for a better and excellent future.

Where there is falsehood there is heartbreak and death.

Where there is falsehood there is hypocrisy.

Where there is falsehood, evil is always present.

Embrace truth.

REFUSE TO BE A PRETENDER

Seek to express yourself from your heart; face the facts of each matter and be real. Never seek to cover up things. 'The things you seek to cover today while you are small will be exposed publicly tomorrow when you are big'. Don't save trouble for your future, deal with it today. Call a spade a spade. Refuse to pretend before man, for it is vain for any man to attempt to pretend before God.

REFUSE TO BE A COWARD

Refuse to be 'man fearer instead be a God fearer'. Those who tremble before God should never tremble before men, for those who tremble before men can never stand upright before God. Cowards die in silence; they are influenced by people's opinions, people's appearances and even by the environment in which they find themselves.

Cowards die with truths they never revealed, with formulas they never experimented; they die with life–giving keys they never used. They die with words they never released because of fear.

Remember, if you close your mouth you close your destiny. Your life and future is in your words. Life and death is in the power of your words.

REFUSE TO BE STUPID

Be filled with God given wisdom. Seek God given secrets for successful living. Refuse to be cheated by life, seek to get the best out of life through faith in Christ. Refuse to be used and abandoned; refuse to be exploited.

Refuse to dwell where you are tolerated, seek to be where you are celebrated. Your future is too precious to be wasted.

Refuse to be devalued by sin, Satan and people. Know who you are in Christ and walk as a child of God.

Remember! You were born to win in life. "There shall not any man be able to stand before thee all the days of thy life: as I was with Moses, so I will be with thee: I will not fail thee, nor forsake thee". Jos 1:5

Abraham was a winner, Moses was a winner, Joshua was a winner even David was a winner. You were born to be part of the winning team. You were not born to be a victim, you were not born to be a disgrace to your community and to God; you were not born to be a failure, but you were born to be a victor in Christ Jesus. Win in life through the power of the Word of God and through the power of the Holy Spirit. God's family is a winning family. Walk daily with winning mentality.

You were born to reign in life

"For the LORD thy God blesseth thee, as he promised thee: and thou shalt lend unto many nations, but thou shalt not borrow; and thou shalt reign over many nations, but they shall not reign over thee". Deut 15:6

We are seated with Christ in heavenly places. We are kings and priests unto our God, halleluiah. Begin to subdue everything that seeks to subdue and to dominate you in any way. In the name of Jesus Christ the Son of God, take authority and be in charge of life, refuse to be ruled by the forces of this world and of the flesh.

Be in charge, be strong and stand in your God given authority. There is a seed of greatness in you. You were designed by God to reign in this life and in eternity with Him. Don't allow the devil to trample on you. Refuse to be pulled around by indecent habits. Take your place and rule by the power of faith in the Son of God. I speak in your life today that all the forces that have dominated and oppressed your life will bow today in the name of Jesus Christ. I reinstate you in your rightful place in life by the apostolic authority in the name of Jesus. Reign in life through Christ Jesus. The enemy will not rule over you anymore.

You were born to live well and healthy in life. "Beloved, I wish above all things that thou mayest prosper and be in health, even as thy soul prospereth". 3Jn 2.

God's will for you is not a sick lifestyle; He desires that you live life fully.

Remember Jesus came to give the 'abundant life'. You need to reject everything that doesn't resemble God from your life. Wellbeing is his eternal will for you; accept it and live by it. Reject all that doesn't make your life better and happier. Believe the Word of God for your life. God's way of life is not for some few special people. His way of life is for all covenant people. Life and health are yours if you are in covenant relationship with Jesus Christ; the only Mediator between man and God.

Confess this out loud over and over

"I will live well and healthy all the days of my life in the name of Jesus Christ".

You were born to live well; it is a matter of choice, choose life today by accepting Jesus Christ as your personal Lord and Savior.

You were born to progress and be successful in life. "The LORD our God spake unto us in Horeb, saying, Ye have dwelt long enough in this mount: Turn you, and take your journey, and go to the mount of the Amorites, and unto all the places nigh thereunto, in the plain, in the hills, and in the vale, and in the south, and by the sea side, to the land of the Canaanites, and unto Lebanon, unto the great river, the river Euphrates. Behold, I have set the land before you: go in and possess the land which the LORD sware unto your fathers, Abraham, Isaac, and Jacob, to give unto them and to their seed after them. Deut 1:6-8.

God said, "Command the children of Israel to move forward". I am here to command you to move forward in every area of your life in Jesus name. Progress in life is God's perfect will for your life; everything that has withheld you from advancing in life is of the enemy.

It is God's will for you to progress in your spiritual life. You should not remain in the same spiritual level. You need to move forward in the knowledge of our Lord Jesus Christ. You need to get deeper in the revelation of the mystery of the glory of the person of Jesus Christ. The Holy Spirit has been waiting to take you in the most incredible journey of your life, the journey into the discovery of the glory of God, in the person of Jesus Christ.

There is need for you to take your steps forward by faith in life. Decide from the inside of you to move forward financially, move forward in ministry, move forward in your projects and investments, and move forward in your career.

Refuse to be stocked by the enemy in the same place for too long. It's time to take steps towards realizing your God given projects. Halleluiah!

You were born to shine in life.

"That ye may be blameless and harmless, the sons of God, without rebuke, in the midst of a crooked and perverse nation, among whom ye shine as lights in the world". Phi 2:15.

This is your season to shine out the beauty of God in you. The Lord wants to be glorified as you shine forth the light in this dark world, praise the Lord. You will shine in your ministry, you will shine in your family, and you must shine in your community in the name of Jesus. Shine out through your excellent performance, shine out through your positive impact in your work place, shine out the glorious light amongst your friends and loved once.

Refuse anything that hinders you from truly shining in life, you were born to be a light in your generation, shine out in Jesus name.

You were born to be rich and wealthy in life

"Praise ye the LORD. Blessed is the man that feareth the LORD, that delighteth greatly in his commandments. His seed shall be mighty upon earth: the generation of the upright shall be blessed. Wealth and riches shall be in his house: and his righteousness endureth for ever". Ps 112:1-3.

Poverty is offensive to man and to God.

Poverty is born out of unbiblical way of life practices.

Poverty is not a blessing from God; it does not have the nature and image of God. It is caused by foolishness, ungodliness, wicked political systems and caused by the enemy of human life; the devil.

Every good and perfect gift comes from above, our heavenly Father is the source of every good thing; He is perfect in goodness and no evil thing proceeds from our God. Wealth is your covenant right as a prophetic seed of Abraham.

You were born to be blessed and be a blessing in life

"And he will love thee, and bless thee, and multiply thee: he will also bless the fruit of thy womb and the fruit of thy land, thy corn, and thy wine, and thine oil, the increase of thy kine, and the flocks of thy sheep, in the land which he sware unto thy fathers to give thee. Thou shalt be blessed above all people: there shall not be male or female barren among you or among your cattle". Deut 7: 13–14.

The Lord wants you to walk in his covenant blessings. His will for you is to be blessed and to become a great blessing to his body the church and to your generation. Know that God's kingdom can never prosper until you prosper, for we are His agents for kingdom building.

You were not born to be an additional trouble and burden to the world; you were not born to be a curse to your family and community. You were born with divine purpose to impact your generation by God's grace. You have a place in God and in all of God's treasures. Reach out by faith for your share of grace for life.

"That which you accept and love you attract"(Mik e Mu rd ock).

You need to know your kingdom inheritance and accept the blessing of the Lord upon your life. You were born to worship God in spirit and in truth in life.

"But the hour cometh, and now is, when the true worshippers shall worship the Father in spirit and in truth: for the Father seeketh such to worship him. God is a Spirit: and they that worship him must worship him in spirit and in truth". Jn 4:23–24.

Halleluiah! You have a reason for existence; you live for God, "all things exist for Him and by Him". Rev 4: 11

You are a worshipping being; refuse to worship any other thing except God the Almighty through His Son Jesus Christ. Refuse to bow to the cravings of the sinful flesh, refuse to bow down to the socio-cultural and political influences on your life.

Refuse to bow to the humanistic and hedonistic ideologies. Refuse to bow to human traditions. You can stand in the midst of pressure as Daniel did in Babylon; you can stand in the midst of opposition as Mordecai did in Persia. He refused to bow to the sinful and ungodly system of his days.

This is your time to prove your love and loyalty for your God. Will you stand as a true worshipper? Or will you join the club of compromisers and continue to dance with the worldly and ungodly systems? Worshiping the only true God is the reason for your existence. Surrender your entire life to God and ask him for strength and grace to be a sincere and dedicated worshipper. Your worship pleases God; God feeds on worship. God's food is true worship, so to say; join the millions of Angels and worship the only true God and Savior Jesus Christ our redeemer. Amen.

If you don't worship him, remember; all creation do worship him day and night. It is your privilege to join all creation to worship the Lord Jesus Christ. It is a wise decision to join all creation to worship and adore the King of kings and the Lord of lords everyday of your life. My family and I have made up our minds to worship the living God, Jesus Christ the Messiah and to serve him with all our dedication.

Refuse to be intimidated by the lies of the devil. You know who you are in God. You are saved and washed by the blood of Jesus Christ. You know your true identity; don't allow any man to look low on you. You are what God's Word says you are, and not what people say or think concerning you. You are more than an opinion; you are a fulfilled prophecy. You are a manifestation of God's vision; you are a divine project with Angels assigned to keep and guide you everyday for the rest of your life. You are created for the glory of God. Are you not important? If not before man, you are important before God. He sent his only begotten Son to die on the cross to save your soul. Halleluiah, worship Him.

It takes a 'Man' to be truthful; it takes a man with a real heart to reject all forms of falsehood. Stress is based upon false pictures and based upon false ideas regarding yourself and the situation you may find yourself in. Stress hates to face the truth, stress hates truth. You need to stand on the truth, love truth, tell yourself the truth and abide in the truth.

Refuse the lies of the devil concerning your life.

Refuse the lies of the enemies regarding your future. Truth brings forth solutions, truth brings healing; your healing depends on your relationship to truth. If you love truth you love life, if you love truth you will live longer. If you hate the truth you love crisis and you unknowing add fuel to the fire burning your soul and fortunes.

Tell yourself the truth; the truth is the Word of God. Tell yourself what the Word of God says.

Refuse thoughts that result to oppression, self degradation and destruction.

Reject thoughts of failure and thoughts of defeat.

Refuse suicidal thoughts. Accept the peace of God in your life in Jesus name. You were not born to be stressed up; you were born to reach out and to help the needy and to be a source of hope to your community. Be stress free. Love truth and live by it, tell your friends nothing but the truth and live by the truth you know.

Refuse to deceive yourself: do what you know is right to do for yourself, to your neighbors and to God. Let your standards be according to divine standards. Don't live in frustration, live life fully in accordance with the Word of peace. If your life's principles are in direct violation to the Word of God, then you have willingly chosen to walk in to afflictions and distress. Your wrong choices will eventually result to wrong, undesirable and uncomfortable end. Godlessness is equal to worthlessness; Worthlessness results to stressfulness. Your true value is in God. You are a child of God, washed and redeemed by the blood of Jesus Christ. You are somebody in God and nobody without God. Be an individual on earth with the joy and blessing of God, the Almighty.

Six things you need in order to be a man or woman of truth

BOLDNESS AND FEARLESSNESS

"For God hath not given us the spirit of fear; but of power, and of love, and of a sound mind", 2Tim 1:7.

Be bold to face the challenges of your life. Be bold to speak out your mind about each subject rather than murmuring in silence. Speak out your ideas and your opinion. Gossipers lack the boldness to speak out directly to the persons concerned.

Reject cowardness and childishness. Be bold, be a man with the freedom to speak out, rather than to die inside in hypocrisy and grumbling. Face every matter wisely and prayerfully with the spirit of love and simplicity.

PERSONAL INTEGRITY

"God forbid that I should justify you, till I die I will not remove my integrity from me", Job 27:5.

Be a man with a sound testimony. Don't live with skeletons in the closet. Have a life free from accusations. You can never stand for truth with personal fears about your secret issues. Fear of being exposed is very destructive. Be free from double personality. Be able to stand before man and God without fear. Walk in integrity, speak with integrity, relate with integrity, and serve God as a man of integrity.

MORAL UPRIGHTNESS

"He that walketh in his uprightness feareth the LORD: but he that is perverse in his ways despiseth him", Pro 14:2.

"Better is the poor that walketh in his uprightness, than he that is perverse in his ways, though he be rich", Pr 28:6.

Immorality is abomination. Immoral people have immoral influence. Immoral people cherish immoral friends and immoral people have immoral atmosphere around them. There is no peace for the immoral, for sin kills. Have a lifestyle of peace and harmony.

Quarreling and fighting is the usual lifestyle of the immoral. Abusive language and insult is their common way of life. Get out of the circle of immoral friends. For you to be a model in society and in the body of Christ, you need to clean up yourself from every form of mess and live with a purpose to affect the world positively. Jesus Christ is able and willing to help you out; just tell him the truth in prayers.

MENTAL SOUNDNESS

"As a man thinketh so is he,' said King Solomon", Pro 23:7.

If you think foolishness you will speak and live foolishly.

If you think greatness you will speak and pursue and walk unto greatness.

If you think childishly, you will speak like a child and live like a child and be immature in your way of life. If you think godly, you will walk godly and will inherit the blessings of the godly.

Be sound in your mind. Feed your mind with sound wisdom from the word of God. Feed your spirit with inspired preaching and sound Biblical teaching.

Keep your mind alive and filled with the Holy Spirit. Always have a healthy mind. Fill your mind with faith and vision. If you think life, you will talk life and appreciate and live life fully.

BE SIMPLE.

"The entrance of thy words giveth light; it giveth understanding unto the simple", Ps 119:130.

Stop complicating life, don't be sophisticated any more. God is a simple God. Anybody can approach him at anytime, if only you have his son as your personal Savior. Take away the barriers you have built to intimidate and to keep people away from you. Jesus was a man for the people. He touched the leprous and ate with the unclean. That is why they had the courage to tell him all the truth. God uses simple people to do great things; history makers are not some super people, but simple individuals with simple background but men of purpose and men of great faith.

Stay humble and available to serve the people around you for the glory and the advancement of the kingdom of God.

BE A CHILD OF GOD

"At the same time came the disciples unto Jesus, saying, 'who is the greatest in the kingdom of heaven? And Jesus called a little child unto him, and set him in the Midst of them; and said, "Verily I say unto you, except ye be converted, and become as little children, ye shall not enter into the Kingdom of heaven. Whosoever therefore shall humble himself as this little child, the same is greatest in the kingdom of heaven. And whosoever shall receive one such little child in my name receiveth me" Matt 18:15.

It is impossible to walk in truth as long as your soul is not saved and delivered from the power of sin. "That which is born of the world is worldly and that which is born of God is Godly". Children of God are born of the Spirit and the nature of God dwells in them: "for if any man be in Christ he is a new creation Old things are passed away and all things have become new" 2 Cor 5:17

A true child of God is inseparable from the truth, for the truth dwells in him. A true child of God has first of all the desire to please God in any given situation and condition. Becoming a child of God has to do with a transformation and a baptism. A baptism that brings to death the flesh and all its cravings and a Baptism that impacts life and power into the spirit of the child of God through a personal walk and intimacy with Jesus Christ. The Holy Spirit baptism is an uncommon experience that breaks and sets free from every form of bondage and addictions. The only person God can trust on earth is his child that is filled with the Holy Spirit. Child of God; make a difference on earth with your lifestyle of truth. Truth heals and truth sets the heart free. Speak truth and live by the truth.

Truth reveals the nature of God and exposes the devil, speak truth.

Truth binds true friends together; truth convicts hypocrites and drives away gossipers. Truth is the quality that every husband seeks from the wife and truth is that quality that every wife seeks in the husband. Are you a man of truth? You can become one today. Ask Jesus to come into your life and ask him to fill you with His nature.

TRUTH WORKS

Truth is what parents seek from their children.
Truth is what the Judges seek to discover.
Truth is what unfair and corrupt politicians hate.
Truth is for real men and women and responsible individuals.
Truth is what the unjust pay to hide.
Truth brings fears to the unjust and frightens the wicked.

Truth is what preachers are called and anointed for, though many have turned their pulpits to social play grounds and political platforms.

Truth is the reason for the existence of the church; the church exists to bring the good news of salvation to the ends of the earth.

Truth hates all forms of falsehood and truth is the determination to restore justice.

Join the truth club today, be born again. Be His disciple and be commissioned for the truth. Truth must have its place in your home for you to stay stress free; a house without truth can never be at peace. The absence of truth is the presence of stress. Truth sets free. Let truth reign in your life and family. Teach your children the precious value of Biblical truth and impart in them the blessed value of truthful living.

Take truth to your work place; refuse to be corrupted by your colleagues. Resist the devil and he will flee from you. Set a standard of truth around you. Let all who know you, know your identity as a truthful person.

Truth will cause you to be identified by God as his faithful servant and God will surely reward your truthfulness in due time.

Truth is the nature of God and all who are godly should worship God in spirit and in truth.

Truth defines true Christianity and reveals true love.

Truth is the spirit of honesty and transparency.

Falsehood and lies separate best friends.

Truth hates craftiness and hypocrisy.

Truth is what you need to speak; meditate upon and live by daily.

Stand on nothing but the truth as you see in the scriptures. Don't allow church Pharisees to pull you into denominational thinking, think scripturally and have the kingdom of God mentality.

Don't die defending your denominational stand, defend the Bible stand. Defend and define the faith according to the scripture and not according to your denominational creeds. Don't die for your denomination or religious institution in the name of God but without God. Die for the truth. Speak truth gently, practice truth sternly and love truth heartily. Bring truth to your friends and loved ones; never allow your friends to corrupt your mind with humanistic thinking and anti Christ spirit. Don't kill your conscience by hardening your heart to do that which your spirit knows right well, to be against God's perfect will for you.

Don't kill your spiritual life through carnality, worldliness practices. Let your friends know your stand; don't compromise in anything that draws you away from God. Share Jesus with your friends, be bold, be strong, be faithful and be truthful. It's time to take the truth of the Word of God to the street as never before; "go ye into all the world and preach the Gospel", were the words of Jesus. Don't be ashamed to testify publicly that you are a new creation.

Keep yourself from anyone who hates the truth. Stick closer to those who delight in nothing but the truth. Those who are willing to face the truth and accept the truth are people who are able to maintain peace and seek reconciliation instead of causing havoc and disunity.

Truth is supposed to be the character and message of the church and of every follower of Jesus Christ.

My prayer today is, "oh Lord raise up men and women who will demonstrate the power of your Word, by making a difference with their lifestyle in our corrupt and perverse society". Where are the Daniels of our day? Daniel made a great difference in Babylon, even though he was but a slave in a foreign nation. He refused the king's provision in order to keep himself from being defiled and corrupted by the king.

Lord, give us men like 'Meshach, Shadrach and Abednego'; men who refused to bow down to Nebuchadnezzar's golden image. They would rather die than bow to a system of oppression and falsehood. Men of truth will not bow to a corrupt system; they stand to make a difference.

Men of truth will not bow to the will of man in contrast to the will of God. Men of truth will not bow to humanistic philosophy. Refuse to bow; it is time to stand and to make the difference.

Don't bow to stress; don't bow to the spirit of quarrels and envy. Your heart was not meant for pain and distress. Let there be a song of praise in your heart today. Let your heart be filled with heavenly melody. You were created to celebrate and to be happy for all that the Lord has done.

CHAPTER FOUR
The Miracles Unity

"Unless you can find some sort of loyalty,
you can not find unity and peace in your active
living".

CHAPTER FOUR
The Miracles of Unity

Hate division; divided opinions leads to confusion, and confusion leads to foolish acts. You need to stay focused on the goals and purpose of your life. Stay united within you. Be one inside, in your mind and spirit. The plan of your enemy is to lead you into confusion in order to cause diverse thoughts and multiple suggestions and opinions in your heart. The moment you allow the devil to cause division in your spirit you are headed for failure.

As long as you hate division, hate conflicts; don't initiate conflicts, seek solutions to the crisis people seek to involve you into. Refuse to walk in division and hate.

Refuse to be confused, stay calm and stay in charge.

Refuse to be desperate, refuse the feeling of frustration. Refuse war and fighting. There is no profit in disputes, disputes gives to hatred and hatred gives birth to birth wickedness. It is foolish to sit down and think on how to hurt your fellow human being because of some disagreement and discrepancy. God is eternally one in perfect unity with Himself. The Father, the Son and the Holy Spirit are never in any form of conflicts.

You should seek to be in perfect peace and harmony with yourself and with your friends. Peace and harmony is more profitable; unity is the spirit of peace. There can never be peace without the presence of unity in concept and in practice.

Today the Lord is calling us to seek peace and to stay in harmony with one another. We can see in our world today that there is no peace due to multitudes of opinions and individuals who seek to gain advantage of others. They press hard for their own ideas and agenda not for the profit of the nations but for their personal interests. Don't seek to kill every other person just to make your way through.

It is time to put aside everything that brings disunity and all that causes conflict and disputes amongst brethren. Learn to share. See to promote unity and not tribal, religious and regional conflicts. We can never be the same or think the same way. We were created differently, let's accept others just the way they are and commit them to God for his grace.

Seek to promote intercultural unity. Denominations can never save any man; it is faith in Jesus Christ that saves. Don't let denominations and various names of churches and ministries divide us any longer. Unity in the truth of the Word of God comes through maturity and revelation by the Holy Spirit. It is time to put aside our traditional beliefs and seek to know the REAL truth, truth according to the whole counsel of God.

So many denominations have held on man made, denominations practices and false biblical beliefs for so many years that they are now ashamed to correct their error and teach the truth to their congregations. It's time to unite in that which is good, and that which is scriptural; no matter who is involved in it. Let us put aside tribalism and nepotism and seek to fulfill the purpose of God in our generation.

True unity begins with one's self, with you. Put yourself together and be at peace with yourself. Stop fighting with yourself; listen to the inner voice within you. Stop the war between your soul and your spirit. Yield to your spirit, as you yield to the Holy Spirit. Your spirit man must be totally yielded to the Holy Spirit for you to have spiritual peace. Hate to be the cause of disorder and disunity. Know that you are not the only wise person on earth. Seek to understand and reason with others.

You can never be right all the time. Admit that you were wrong and be sorry for your mistakes. Don't be the cause of family disorder, seek to unite and seek to bring peace.

"Blessed are the peacemakers for they shall be called the sons of God", Matt 5:9

Unity brings progress; you can never have progress in your personal life in disunity and conflicts. And there cannot be effective and continuous community development as long as the counselors are in disunity. The simple secret of progress is unity in purpose. Churches fail to grow due to internal divisions; many come together but in total different camps. Nobody will ever invest in a place filled with confusion and lack of purpose. One of the greatest weapons the devil uses against the church is division. Divided church elders will produce a multiparty church. A multiparty church will have unaccomplished diverse visions; some will be dancing to the tone of the pastor, some to the tone of the deacons and some after the elders.

Is Christ divided? Why is there so much division and fighting among Christian denominations? Today so many are fighting for recognition, others for promotion and popularity. While some are fighting for church money, what a disgrace! The Church of God is meant to be a place for prayers, a house for worship and not a business center. Stop using God's name to make wealth for yourself in the name of church. If God has not called you, then Satan has called and assigned you to rob the saints of God; repent before it's too late. God have mercy.

Many families are suffering because of the demon of division and disunity; many have even killed their relatives because of misunderstanding. There is no profit in disunity. Nations are fighting against nations because of differences in opinions. There is war today in many nations just because somebody's ideas were not accepted. Therefore he turns to gather the 'sons of Belial' to fight for him; the end result will be killing innocent souls. My dear friend; if you want to fight, fight using your pen and your words and fight for the right cause. Fight for true freedom, fight for love and peace; fight against wickedness, fight against all forms of evil and occult practices. Resist the devil and he will flee. Remember that the weapons of our warfare are not carnal but they are Mighty through God.

It is time to stand against disunity and confusion. Fight for oneness amongst brethren; fight for a united force to fight against the ills of society. This is your time to take action and unite for the building of the kingdom of God in your local area. Cause God's kingdom to prosper in your community.

The unity of your family is the prosperity of your family. The unity of the church is the growth and expansion of the church of God. The unity of your community is its development.

Unite in purpose and in common actions towards community development. Unite in community projects that are aimed at bringing tangible improvements in the lives of people.

THE POWER AND POSITIVE EFFECTS OF TRUE UNITY

What does it take to fly a plane? It takes united efforts and skillful contributions. There is always so much chaos when one department fails to fulfill its role efficiently. The pilots cannot fly any plane safely without good communications with the control tower.

The pilots will never be safe and satisfied to take off, if they are not sure of the safety and soundness of the engines of the plane. The pilots are not the ones responsible for the fueling and loading and off loading of the luggage. Some people must be very committed for the assurance that the right bag is loaded to the right plane before it takes off. You see that it has to do with united force and commitment of so many departments for a plane to fly safely.

You can never succeed in any major project that God has given you except you have dedicated and skillful individuals who are willing to join hands with you for the common goal; in a true spirit of unity to realize the God given project. Many have failed in life because they had evil people around their projects and ministries, people who came with selfish intentions to divide and to cause confusion for personal interest.

Many Churches cannot grow because everybody has his or her own vision and secret ambition. Your church or ministry would grow more when every department within the church seeks to fulfill the general vision of the church in its own unique way.

A church may have fifty or more departments, but with one goal and a common vision as a body. The body of Church of God is sick today in many nations of the world because the various Christian bodies or denominations have lost their focus. Therefore their followers have no purpose and have nothing to do after being saved except to pay tithes and offerings and If you are faithful in tithes and offerings then you are a good Christian, even though you are idling in the church. For the church to be alive and effective there must be a clear vision and clear understanding to all the members of the vision and mission of the congregation.

The church as a family of God's precious people is suffering from dead heads. Leaders that have nothing more to do than to work hard to raise funds for their retirement can never be instruments for the end time restoration and great awakening of the church. Children of God need a fresh vision and a fresh word from the throne room of God for the purpose of fulfilling our end time divine assignment.

Where there is no purpose and commission to fulfill, there can be no motivation for the end time harvest. Division comes in when there is a need for actions towards realizing a given goal. Division comes in when there are contrary views from that of the vision bearer. Divisions come in when opinions are diverse and the leadership authority is challenged. To be stress free means to be in unity even though with some areas of disagreement. It is possible to disagree and still work for the common good.

It is never possible to be in total agreement with any human being on earth that has a free mind and a mouth and the right to be different. The only person that will ever be in total agreement with your will is a corpse. We might disagree on where to spend our holidays and still be in unity, knowing that we will get the right conclusion with time.

To live stress free means to gain maturity in dealing with the different challenges, opinions and behaviors and responses of other people. Maturity has to do with the right to be different, in thinking, in actions and in speech. It has to do with the freedom to express yourself wherever you are without fear and intimidation.

Maturity has to do with accepting other people for who they are and not trying to make every person your duplicate. The world would be a terrible place to live in if everybody thought alike and acted the same all the time. It is a blessing to celebrate our uniqueness.

There should be unity in diversity. The body of Christ has many gifts and operations of the Spirit in order to meet variety of human needs, yet by the same Spirit. It took unity of skills to build the tabernacle in the wilderness. For God gave some individuals special ability just for specific assignments. Accept people with their differences.

CHAPTER FIVE
The Grace Of Appreciation

"We tend to forget that happiness doesn't come as a result of getting something we don't have, but rather of recognizing and appreciating what we do have".

Frederick Keonig

CHAPTER FIVE
THE GRACE OF APPRECIATION

Everybody loves to be appreciated; appreciation is fuel for motivation. Appreciation inspires people to do better. Cheer up some one who is downcast and has lost hope in life and you will restore life and strength for a new beginning. God is seeking for men and women with an appreciative heart, men that would be thankful for the air they breathe, men that would be thankful for the life and health they have, men that would be thankful to God for being able to have a job. Be full of thanksgiving, for thanksgiving opens new doors for greater opportunities.

Many are filled with bitterness and complain. They seem to see nothing good in life, they grumble and hate. Begin to see the difference in you, see how God has been good to you; see so many around you that have not even one tenth of all that you have in life. See how God has kept you from being a victim to some serious disaster that could have crippled your whole life. See the goodness of God surrounding your daily life. Stop complaining, start appreciating, and stop grumbling, start praising God.

Begin to appreciate others for a job well done; give somebody a reason to smile by telling him or her, "am proud of you, you are wonderful; I thank God for you, if not of you…" When you appreciate, you heal hearts from the feeling of worthlessness, and you take away stress and give people a reason to be relaxed in mind. Take away tension and seek to give people a reason to love life, make life beautiful and enjoyable. Appreciate your friends for their love and concern. Thank them for being there for you; tell them how much you value their relationship and company.

Lack of appreciation can cause discouragement and to those who are not yet mature; it can even cause them to give up on some important virtues. Lack of the spirit of appreciation can be caused by self pride and the feeling that you can do it with or without any person. For those who think they don't need any person, they also don't see the need to be thankful for the favor done to them. I have come to learn that nobody can live without the assistance of another person, even if you are a medical doctor, you still will need another medical doctor to consult.

Be thankful, be grateful and learn to appreciate. Appreciate your children for being there for you and for their services. Say thank you to your children for services rendered. Learn to appreciate in words and in kind. You can show appreciation by giving a seasonal gift, or by writing a card to some loved ones. Just do it in your own way; in all, do show appreciation without reservation and without prejudice. When you learn to appreciate others, you set yourself free from the temptation of self glory and from the spirit of envy. Jealousy cannot stay in the heart of someone who seeks to cheer up others and someone who appreciates and is thankful for the blessing he receives from the lives and ministries of others.

Stress gives birth to harsh words; stress is the mother of anger and the father of conflicts. People fight because they are stressed up within and have no peace and hope for an alternative way out. Don't give yourself over to stress; give yourself over to the Lord Jesus Christ. Stress kills, stress leads unto various health issues. Relax your mind, decide to live stress free and have a healthy heart. Let go of the pains of your past, learn to say well done, thank you please, I am very sorry, forgive me etc. When you cause others to be happy, you indirectly cause yourself to be happy. You will harvest the happiness that you sow in the lives of others. The pains you cause others to go through in life, after they must have gone through it, it will in turn find you out except you deal with in repentance before the Lord.

Appreciate peace, appreciate the comfort of others and appreciate the prosperity and success of others. Wish others good success and God's blessing, have a good heart towards people.

Goodness will always follow those who wish goodness for others, and wickedness will be the portion of the wicked. A wicked young man will certainly have an undesirable old age except he or she turns to the Lord for salvation. The respect you give to others will be multiplied and given back to you in due time.

Don't allow people to push you into a life of fleshly competing with others, for many are bound by the force of material competition or financial competition. Competition always leads to envy and jealousy. Seek God for all that he has for you; let others have their lives. Be yourself; seek God for his blessing, for his glory alone and not for a show up. Be satisfied with all that God has blessed you with, for God has created you in a unique way. Don't mess up your mind; give no place for the devil; be stress free, appreciate.

LORD THANK YOU

"Today in a bus, I saw a lovely girl with golden hair. I envied her; she seemed so beautiful and wished I were as fair. When suddenly she rose to leave, I saw her hobble down the aisle. She had one leg and wore a crutch; and as she passed a smile."

"Oh God, forgive me, I have two legs; I should be grateful and thankful to you."

Then I stopped to buy some candy. The lad who sold them had such charm; I talked with him, he seemed so glad. And as I left he said to me, "I thank you; you have been so kind, it's nice to talk with folks like you". "You see" he said "I am blind." Oh God, forgive me, I have two eyes, I should be grateful and thankful to you. Later, as I walked down the street, I saw a child with blue eyes. He stood and watched the others play. It seemed he knew not what to do. I stopped a moment and then I said, "Why don't you join the others dear?" He looked ahead without a word, and then I knew, he could not hear. Oh

God, forgive me, I have two ears, I should be grateful and thankful to you.

With legs to take me where I'd go, with eyes to see the sunset's glow, with ears to hear what I would know. Oh God, forgive me, I'm blessed indeed, thank you Lord".

By Evan Krivohlaveh Ben.

Have you said thank you today? To friends who have been so gracious and kind to you. Have you said thank you today? To parents who laid down their everything to take good care and to guide you as a child. Have you said thank you today to God the Almighty, through whom and by whom and for whom we live? Without Him there is no life; for He is the source of life and all blessings.

Be thankful, be gracious and be kind.

CHAPTER SIX
Speak To My Heart

"One of the hardest things in life is having words in your heart that you can't utter".
James Earl Jones.

CHAPTER SIX
SPEAK TO MY HEART

You were born to share and to have fellowship with others. You are not complete without others. Adam was never complete without Eve; God is not complete without Angels and man to communicate with. You can never be complete without relating to other people in love and friendliness. Loneliness most of the time is a product of lack of good communication. The enemy's assignment is to cause a breach in communication, and then destroy fellowship and companionship. You were not created to live lonely. You exist because others do exist and for your existence to be meaningful and exciting, you need to seek to relate well with others that God has placed around you.

You can not be a monk, {one that is withdrawn from society} and seek to change the world; you change people by relating to people, showing people your concern and reaching out to touch them in their area of pain. You exist to meet someone's need. All that you are; all that you have and all that you know are not for yourself. You exist to provide solutions around you by responding in love to others.

You exist to make others complete and you are complete with others around you. How long will you survive if you were left alone on earth? Just imagine living with no one to talk to, with nowhere to visit, with no one to walk with. Everybody needs someone to share with. You need someone to feel with you; you need someone to encourage and to cheer you up along life's journey.

Good communication brings order and harmony in our world. Just imagine a world without a means of information. Imagine an airport without a means of communication. Airplanes cannot fly without good communication. Can you imagine what would happen if there is communication breakdown on our railway stations? Can you imagine the atmosphere in a home with breakdown in communication? Can you imagine the devastating effects of breakdown in communication with God in the lives of Adam and Eve? Good friends became enemies overnight.

How many homes have severe disorder today due to lack of communication? I see so many sick children on our streets, children sick of the lack of attention, children sick in their hearts because of emotionally sick homes and psychologically sick parents. Please decide to restore communication today with your spouse, your friends or colleague in the name of Jesus Christ. And you will see the great difference it will make. Communication brings order.

Unresolved lack in communication between political parties will always result to more tensions that do hinder our national progress and prosperity. There will be fewer wars of only leaders can seat down and talk. God gave us the ability to resolve our differences through talking, expressing our feelings and opinions through dialogue.

Talk instead of fighting; talk instead of hating and talk instead of separation. Bring the matter to the table and let's examine it peacefully and in prayers. Don't run away when you are hurt, express yourself and let's seek a common solution.

The only way to bring restoration and healing in your broken relationship is to reach out and begin to talk again even though it hurts.

I pray and declare today in the name of Jesus Christ. Let there be order in your marriage; let there be restored peace in your ministry; let there be sweetness and harmony again in your life; just talk things out in Jesus might name.

Good Communication will result to unity, and tension is eased through peaceful communication. Lack of communication is a breeding ground for every wrong seed from the devil in your mind. You should know that in division and separation we can never prosper in one personal and family life. Let us seek unity through the freedom to share and talk even in painful moments. Through your restored communication you will doubtful bring understanding and clarifications to issues that have been setting you apart for so long. Let's talk heart to heart and let's heal our families and nation.

Many churches are sick because of breach in communication between the leadership team and the senior. The only way to stop church gossip is by timely communication with the church on issues facing to the church. The church is a place of fellowship with God and with one another. Let there be freedom to share and to live as a family in Christ Jesus. Heal the wounds by talking and sharing with one another through the love of God.

I do advise couples to keep each other informed of their financial situations, lack of financial and sexual communication are the major reasons for marital crimes and marriage breakdowns. The hiding from one another should be over, talk, share and live the life you dreamed of by choice. It is time you mature and face the fact that there cannot be prosperity until you both come together financially for the common good of the family. The family's progress is based on unity through communication and planning together. "For two shall become one", says the Scriptures.

Marriage has to do with oneness and intimacy in every area. May God bring deliverance from divisions and financial and sexual fights in the name of Jesus Christ. True communication develops intimacy. Friendship without communication will not last. It takes communication to develop trust and confidence in one another. Lovers talk to each other; friends share deep secrets together. It is time to make Jesus your personal friend. Talk with him in prayers and spend time in worshiping him. Seek to develop your love relationship with Jesus Christ and the Holy Spirit. Jesus Christ wants you to be his personal friend.

What a privilege to be a friend of God! Tell him all about your life. Tell him, you love him and just love to spend time alone with him. You develop intimacy as you withdraw yourself from all the chores of daily life to spend adequate time alone with your loved one. It is necessary to spend time with your most special one; Jesus Christ your Savior and Lord. Intimacy has to do with love from your innermost heart.

There is no way you can ever live stress free with out sincere love for man and for God. Don't allow anything rob you from the freedom of communicating with the people God has connected you with in life.

HINDRANCES TO GOOD COMMUNICATION

UNFORGIVING

"So shall ye say unto Joseph, Forgive, I pray thee now, the trespass of thy brethren, and their sin; for they did unto thee evil: and now, we pray thee, forgive the trespass of the servants of the God of thy father'. And Joseph wept when they spake unto him". Gen 50:17.

It is impossible to share deep intimacy with grudge and unforgiving spirit. Unforgiving spirit is demonic and leads unto deep bondage. Thank God for Joseph, for he forgave his brothers for their evil. True freedom begins with your inner man releasing people and hurt from your heart. Unforgiving is the number one hindrance to intimacy and good communication. Be free from the power of unforgiving spirit in Jesus name.

LACK OF TRUTHFULNESS

"Send one of you, and let him fetch your brother, and ye shall be kept in prison, that your words may be proved, whether there be any truth in you: or else by the life of Pharaoh surely ye are spies". Gen 42:16.

There is no way to talk freely with issues you are afraid to deal with. Lack of truthfulness is the father and mother of hypocrisy; hypocrisy gives birth to insincerity and craftiness.

Be truthful and share with others from the depth of your heart. Let your friends know exactly who you are; stop hiding your true self; friendliness has to do with exposing one's self to another in love. It has to do with opening up of one's self; revealing yourself. Your true friend has to know the ugly and the good side of you. That is why Jesus Christ came to make us all anew, no matter what your past might have been; in Christ we are all new creation.

This is the joy of our new life, all things have become new. My past is over, Halleluiah. I am not ashamed to confess my sins publicly, for Jesus Christ my Savior did not die in secret but he died publicly on the cross on top of the mountain for the whole world to see. Don't be ashamed any more of your sinful past, it is all over. The Christ in you has cleansed and redeemed you from the curse of sin and death. You are now a child of God, with heaven as your goal. Praise the Lord.

GOSSIP AND FALSE ACCUSATIONS

"These six things doth the LORD hate: yea, seven are an abomination unto him: A proud look, a lying tongue, and hands that shed innocent blood. A heart that deviseth wicked imaginations, feet that be swift in running to mischief. A false witness that speaketh lies and he that soweth discord among brethren". Pro 6:16:19.

Gossip is one of the major root causes of discord and hatred amongst brethren. It is very difficult to flow in the spirit with people of whom you have heard negative stories concerning them; and it is not possible to be in deep friendship with people who gossip about you. For those who speak evil concerning you behind your back are capable of planning even your death. There is a natural tendency to avoid those whom you know do go about your name falsely. Avoid gossip and refrain from issues which you don't have full evidence to back you up.

Do not be the cause of tension and misunderstanding.

Do not be a part of a gossip team; do not be the cause of stress in the family and the community. Be a channel of peace, heals hearts.

THE SPIRIT OF LORDSHIP

"And there was also a strife among them, which of them should be accounted the greatest'. 26. "But ye shall not be so: but he that is greatest among you let him be as the younger; and he that is chief, as he that doth serve". LK 22:24.

Nobody will seek a relationship where his or her values are not respected.

Nobody wants to be lorded upon. Nobody wants to be controlled and manipulated.

We need friends for mutual fellowship not for lordship. For communication to be effective there should be an atmosphere of equality and dependency upon one another. We learn from each other and we do need each other's contribution for effective communication and fellowship.

The spirit of superiority and self importance drive away people, while the nature of simplicity and gentleness attracts people. Husbands are not the gods and the lords of the family but instead they are to be the heads of the family in terms of responsibility and administration; submitting to one another in love.

FAMILY COMMUNICATION

"A new commandment I give unto you, that ye love one another as I have loved you; that ye also love one another". John 13:34.

"This is my commandment, that ye love one another as I have loved you". John 15:12.

"These things I command you, that ye love one another". John 15:17.

"Owe no man anything, but to love one another: for he that loveth another hath fulfilled the law". Rom 13:8.

"But as touching brotherly love ye need not that I write unto you: for ye yourselves are taught of God to love one another". 1Th 4:9.

For a family to be healthy and happy there must be freedom of expression and freedom to play. Many wives in some of our cultures have been reduced to 'house workers'. They are responsible for all household duties while husbands patrol as little home lords waiting for food to be served. They have no relationship with the man of the house called the, 'husband'.

It is very sad that even in this century they are still cultures where women have no right to share their opinions regarding family matters or social issues. What the men expect from their wives is for them to follow instructions and their commandments. Unfortunately, this is not marriage as God intended for his children. Marriage is a relationship of friendship and oneness and not servant hood.

You seek for a husband or wife because you need a special friend to share with for life. You long for someone to invest your love and to care for as long as God gives you life. May God fulfill your heart's desire in restoring love and true oneness in your life and family, in the name of Jesus Christ.

I pray that God will visit your home and transform things in Jesus name. May you enter into a new love relationship with your spouse in the name of Jesus Christ. May you enjoy your choice of husband or wife and may your family be a great blessing in Jesus Name.

CHAPTER SEVEN

The Force Of Faith

"Faith makes all things possible.... love makes all things easy."

Unknown

CHAPTER SEVEN
THE FORCE OF FAITH

Faith is what it takes to be what God wants us to be.

Faith is what I need in order to be what God's Word says I should be.

Faith is what it takes in order to reject all that which is not of God and all that which is not from God.

Faith is what you need in order to receive all that is of God and all that is from God, Halleluiah.

Faith is what it takes to become your dream.

Faith and wisdom is what you need to overcome vision and destiny killers. Faith is what it takes in order to realize the result of your prayer.

Faith is what it takes to become what you have believed.

Faith is what it takes to transform hopeless situations.

Faith is what it takes to bring to life dead situations.

Faith is not for some privileged few, faith is for whosoever wills.

Faith means believing God, accepting his Word as it is written and living by it.

Arise in your heart with aggressive faith for a new beginning. It is possible; say with me aloud, it is possible; you can transform your situation through simple faith in God's Word.

FAITH FOR YOUR PERSONAL BREAKTHROUGH IN LIFE

The story of your life will never be a pleasant one until you get hold of the power of faith and walking by it.

It will take faith for you to step out into all that God has for you. God had already designed your breakthrough and it is waiting for you to press on for it by faith.

It will take a surrendering to God and to all that God has said. It will take accepting the Word of God as a fool: even though you don't understand how and when, yet believing it and knowing with full assurance that the promise will certainly manifest for you exactly as God has said.

The dream of your heart is possible to become a testimony. That visions and projections of your heart were not just meant to be written down but to be pursued by faith. Today, begin to enlist every area in which you need a personal breakthrough for a new beginning and release your faith for them. Look for Bible promises that are related to the vision and projections of your life and begin to confess and declare them. Begin to begin to paint the pictures of your expected future in your mind. Let them become tangible visible images in your mind. Accept it as a done deal and surrender it to God for a miracle and rest in faith without fear.

Whatever breakthrough may mean for you, I have come to tell you that faith says it is possible to see it happen. It happened to Abraham. It can happen to you. It happened to Joseph in Egypt it can happen to you. It happened to me and changed my platform in life and I know it will manifest for your testimony. The same God that changed the story of Joseph changed my personal story and this is the season for your breakthrough. Do you believe it? Breakthrough is knocking at your door, believe it, accept it, confess it and step into it and welcome in by faith in Jesus name.

Whatever you may be believing God for, begin to praise him for it. You have prayed enough. Begin to praise God and celebrate your testimony by faith. Begin to give him glory for doing it. Begin to prepare your testimonial offering. See it, feel it, touch it by faith and hand it to God for the manifestation. Halleluiah!

FAITH FOR UNCOMMON SUCCESS

Success is accomplishing what you were created to be and to do. Uncommon success is possible; do you believe you were born to be successful? Today begin to deal with the root of the failures in your life. God's eternal desire is to see you successful in every area of your life, for He is glorified in your success.

No parent will ever celebrate the failure of his or her children; failures bring shame to the family. You were not born to bring shame; your life must bring a smile to your parents and to your God. These are some common root causes of failure.

SIN

When I think of these biblical names, I think of people who failed because of sin; Adam and Eve; Reuben, Samson the long hair prophet, King Saul, Absalom, Ananias and Sapphira, Judas, Etc…

Many of our potential youths have destroyed their lives and future because they chose the life of crime and disorder. Many of our Anointed Gospel ministers have allowed sin to soak out the unction of the Holy Spirit from their lives and sin has caused many to turn the pulpit to a playground.

Sin has caused many African heads of state to do all they can to die in power because of fear. They know that if they lose the throne they will be brought to justice for all the inhuman acts they have committed.

Sin has caused many religious leaders to become engaged in 'mafia' because of the desire to gain wealth in an unscriptural manner. Many because of the struggle for position and promotion have become sorcerers and religious wizards. They are ready to kill anybody that dares to stand on their way. The church has become the den of charismatic robbers.

Sin has caused the church of today to become a religious institution instead of the voice of God for the nations. My prayer today is "oh Lord; bring back your glory, restore your tangible presence to your church again. Revive us again and baptize your people with the baptism of the fear of God."

Remember, sinful lifestyle brings unnecessary pain and many regrets in life

"Before I was afflicted I went astray: but now have I kept thy word". Ps 119:67.

UNBELIEF

Yesterday, I preached in an Italian church in Torino-Italy; after preaching for some forty-five minutes the Holy Spirit led me to stop and call a lady from the congregation and to ask her some questions. So I asked her the first question, "Have you given your life to Jesus?" Her answer was no. Then I asked her the second question, "Would you like to receive Jesus Christ as your personal Lord and Savior?" Surprisingly, she said no. I then proceeded with the third question, "Why won't you receive Jesus Christ?" And her response was "because I don't know him". "Would you like to know him personally?" and she said no.

All these happened in the church you know; she was a church member but interestingly not for Jesus Christ.

How can you ever help someone to know Jesus who does not want to? The only thing to do is to pray for God to visit them in his own way and in his own time. Unbelief is lack of faith in God. I ask a receptionist in a hotel in Geneva, Italy, "Do you believe in Jesus Christ?" Her response was, "I don't believe in anything. I put my faith in nothing". This is what we call unbelief, lack of faith in the Word of God, and consequently lack of faith in God.

Unbelief keeps men and women from the benefits of the sacrificial blood of Jesus Christ on the cross of Calvary. Unbelief keeps people from partaking in the blessings of the grace of God.

Unbelief is one of the root causes of frustration and depression. When a man chooses to believe God by believing His Word, he has chosen to connect himself with the power of God, the Almighty for supernatural interventions and divine assistance.

Many have hardened their hearts against the Word of God because of their personal painful experiences with religious people that malrepresented the church and the image of God. Nevertheless God is God and His Word remains infallible. He is the same forevermore and blessed are those who love and believe in him. Faith in God produces a people of hope and assured future. Unbelief produces a people with a confused, stressful and vague future; for the only hope of the world is God's sure Word. Remember; lack of faith is foolishness, for only fools say there is no God.

"Well; because of unbelief they were broken off and thou standest by faith. Be not high minded, but fear" Rom 11:20.

INDECISION

Many fail because they are unable to make serious decisions. They have no power to decide; they are what the bible calls, coward. Parents, friends and the fear of people rule them. They are too concerned about people's opinion about them; they are constantly struggling with what people think or are saying concerning them. Eventually they become slaves of people and too afraid to make personal decisions. Success has to do with decision making and responding to the convictions of your inner man as led by the Holy Spirit within you. Success has to do with taking initiatives that result to great breakthroughs in life.

It will take a man or woman with a decisive heart to walk in the Anointing. It takes a decision to live in truth and holiness; it demands a conscious decision to live in this sinful world untouched and uncorrupt by the spirit of this world. It will take your decision to live a stress free life. Happiness and success is for men and women with a heart of wisdom, who take serious decisions to create a better future.

"Multitudes, multitudes in the valley of decision: for the day of the LORD is near in the valley of decision". Joel 3:14.

WRONG FRIENDS

I love everybody but I don't make friends with everybody. Remember Samson and Delilah, Samson became blind and ended up killing himself because he was in love with the wrong person. Keep yourself far from betrayers and far from gain seekers. Ask the Holy Spirit to link you with your God-given friends; there is no more time to waste with purposeless individuals and with antichrist inspired individuals.

This is the time to walk with people of faith and people with a desire to fulfill their God-given assignment. It is time to take that decision to separate from some of your friends that are negative force in your life. Any friend that does not contribute positively towards your growth, your prosperity and your personal advancement and enrichment is not worth keeping. Any friend that does not contribute towards your peace and successful living is an enemy in sheep clothing.

We are commissioned to minister to people, regardless of their lifestyle but never make a 'stranger' your intimate friend. Build relationship with the spirit of discernment. Give yourself time to know the person you are dealing with or you might put yourself in great difficulties. Don't ruin your life by linking up with the wrong team. Your life is too precious to waste with idle people; seek to make the best out of life. Choose your friends prayerfully and wisely.

"Be not deceived: evil communications corrupt good manners". 1Cor 15:33.

UNTEACHABLE SPIRIT

He who refuses to learn has refused to succeed. 'Iron sharpens iron' un-teachable spirit is born out of self pride and the thought of being better than others. The wise seeks to increase in knowledge by seeking to learn all that he needs to know from every possible source. Ignorant people spend their time arguing rather than learning. Have a teachable spirit; be ready to learn even from your children. A person who is ready to learn will receive godly counsel for a better life and future.

"If they obey and serve him, they shall spend their days in prosperity and their years in pleasures". Job 36:11.

LAZINESS

A lazy man has no future.

A lazy person seeks to harvest where he has not sown.

A lazy woman can never be a good wife.

A lazy husband will never be able to pay his bills.

A lazy student has already decided to fail.

A lazy businessman will end up in severe debts.

A lazy pastor's message will always be based on story telling and on tithes and offerings and seed sowing. Instead of seeking to reach more people and building their faith in the word, he settles down to draining everything from the few faithful members.

If you fail to sow your seeds while you are young; you should be ready to have no harvest in your old age.

Let us examine what the wise man Solomon wrote regarding laziness or sluggishness.

"Go to the ant, thou sluggard; consider her ways, and be wise" Pr 6:6. "How long wilt thou sleep, O sluggard? When wilt thou arise out of thy sleep"? Pr 6:9. "As vinegar to the teeth, and as smoke to the eyes, so is the sluggard to them that send him". Pr 10:26.

"The soul of the sluggard desireth, and hath nothing: but the soul of the diligent shall be made fat". Pr 13:4.

"The sluggard will not plow by reason of the cold; therefore shall he beg in harvest, and have nothing". Pr 20:4.

"The sluggard is wiser in his own conceit than seven men that can render a reason". Pr 26:16.

LACK OF WISDOM
You need Godly wisdom for:

- Personal establishment
- Business development
- Financial management
- Ministerial success
- Marital success
- Advancement and promotion
- Happy and victorious living
- Successful investment
- Spiritual growth and stability
- Healthy living
- Stress free life
- Management of divine opportunities, Etc.

"For the LORD giveth wisdom: out of his mouth cometh knowledge and understanding". Pr 2:6.

"He layeth up sound wisdom for the righteous: he is a buckler to them that walk uprightly". Pr 2:7.

"When wisdom entereth into thine heart and knowledge is pleasant unto thy soul". Pr 2:10.

WISDOM HAS TO DO WITH
- Right ideas
- Right decisions
- Right words
- Right choices
- Right actions
- Right timing

- Right judgment and discernment
- Right associations and partnership
- Right heart condition

It is very difficult for a wise man to be a failure in life. It is a curse for a wise man to live in poverty. It is very difficult for a wise man to live in defeats. It is very difficult for a real wise man to refuse Jesus Christ as personal Lord and Savior. It is very difficult for a wise man to live in confusion.

May the wisdom of God cause you to walk in perfect order, peace and excellence in the name of Jesus Christ the son of God. A wise man is not troubled in the face of trouble because he knows there is always a way out for every form of trouble. A man of faith is stirred up in the face of pressures; because he knows that his God will surely show up for a miracle. Halleluiah!

You need faith for your advancement and promotion. "For promotion cometh neither from the east, nor from the west, nor from the south. But God is the judge: he putteth down one, and setteth up another". Ps 75:6-7. "And the LORD said unto Moses, 'Wherefore criest thou unto me? Speak unto the children of Israel that they go forward". Exo 14:15.

It's time for you to move forward in every area of your life. I speak in your life today that nothing will keep you from your God given place in life, in the name of Jesus Christ. The will of God is for you to advance in your area of calling, advance in your ministry, advance in your education, advance in your business, etc.

This is your time to move forward and higher by the power of the grace of God. Don't allow the lies of the enemy to keep you from moving forward in life; the devil wants to see you stagnant and ineffective in life. This is never God's plan for your life, refuse the lies of the enemy and build up your faith for your advancement and promotion in life. My Father died when I was just twelve years of age. I had just spent three months in my first year in secondary school when I lost my Dad.

My mother was simply a housewife who fully depended on her farm for daily bread. She had nothing to take care of us. I was the least of five living siblings and all my brothers and sisters were all struggling for their own survival, we had already lost a sister and my direct junior brother. I made up my mind that hardship will never stop my destiny; I decided to believe God for a blessed future. In the midst of poverty I made up my mind to believe for an uncommon future. Today I am a blessing to the nations of the world. Many are calling and requesting for my books from different nations to God be all the glory.

Don't give up on your vision; keep your faith alive in the power of the name of Jesus Christ. Day by day move forward towards fulfilling the vision of your life. Refuse to be stressed out, be stress free to reign in life with Christ Jesus.

FAITH FOR YOUR PROSPERITY

"And his master saw that the LORD was with him, and that the LORD made all that he did to prosper in his hand". Gen 39:3.

"Then answered I them, and said unto them, 'The God of heaven, he will prosper us; therefore we his servants will arise and build: but ye have no portion, nor right, nor memorial in Jerusalem". Neh 2:20.

It will be well with you in Christ Jesus; the heart of God is beating for your wellbeing. God is never pleased when you are in pain and in distress. God wants life to be a blessing for you. Remember, when sin came, it brought with it all the reasons and causes for adversity; when righteousness comes through the knowledge of Jesus Christ the only Son of God, it brings with it all the blessings of the second Adam, Jesus Christ the righteous.

Today you have the choice to make, either to walk under the curse of sin or to walk under the new covenant of the blood of Jesus Christ. For the blood of Jesus Christ has the eternal power to destroy all the effects of sin and to restore all that the devil stole from the fallen man. As for my family and I, we chose to live in Christ and to prosper according to his eternal and unchangeable Word. "It is well with the righteous", says the Word of the Lord; I believe it and I accept it for my descendants and I. What about you? Have faith for your prosperity.

I believe in the God that prospers, and I am a prosperous servant of God through faith in His covenant Word. True prosperity has to do with the wellbeing of your body, soul and spirit. It is impossible to be blessed by God and not prosper. It is impossible to be favored by God and live in desperation. It is impossible for a wise man to die in failure. Godly Wisdom will always find a way out of the mess. You may be going through the dark valley of the shadows of death and facing the mountains and the storms of life; but you will end up with a great testimony because you walk and believe in the covenant Word of God for your life.

Confess after me out aloud, "I was born to prosper for the advancement of the kingdom of God on earth in Jesus name".

FAITH FOR YOUR WEDDING

"And Isaac went out to meditate in the field at the eventide: and he lifted up his eyes and saw, and behold the camels were coming. And Rebekah lifted up her eyes, and when she saw Isaac, she lighted off the camel. For she had said unto the servant, 'what man is this that walketh in the field to meet us'? And the servant had said it is my master: therefore she took a Veil, and covered herself". Gen 24:63-65.

Faithful child of God; nothing will stop you from meeting your God-given spouse. Stand your ground in faith in the word of God for your destiny. Stand on your covenant with God for your descendants. It might delay but wait for it with covenant faith. Bless the Lord for your husband and children; bless the Lord that nothing would ever break your marriage and nothing will stop your family prosperity.

FAITH FOR YOUR HEALING

"And ye shall serve the LORD your God, and he shall bless thy bread, and thy water; and I will take sickness away from the midst of thee". Ex 23:25.

"But unto you that fear my name shall the Sun of righteousness arise with healing in his wings; and ye shall go forth, and grow up as calves of the stall". Mal 4:2. "And Jesus went about all Galilee, teaching in their synagogues, and preaching the gospel of the kingdom, and healing all manner of sickness and all manner of disease among the people". Mt 4:23. "Behold, I will bring it health and cure, and I will cure them, and will reveal unto them the abundance of peace and truth". Jer 33:6.

There is divine provision for your healing today; you can receive your healing now. Jesus Christ has made provision for your health. Receive healing for your broken and wounded heart. Receive healing and restoration for your spiritual life. Receive healing for your broken marriage and family. Receive healing from hopelessness and confusion. Receive healing from the effects of a sinful life and from every form of addiction. Receive healing from loneliness and bitterness of heart. Receive healing for every financial crisis and bondage you may be in today. Today he is willing to heal your life and ministry, if only you can humble yourself and turn to Him with all your heart.

Jesus understands the struggles in your heart, he shed his precious blood just for you; He wants you completely healed and sound, body, soul and spirit. Begin to confess your healing and denounce every negative condition from your life. For we live by faith and not by sight. Begin to see yourself healed and totally set free from the power of infirmity in Jesus mighty name. "He sent his word, and healed them, and delivered them from their destructions". Ps 107:20. "I taught Ephraim also to go, taking them by their arms; but they knew not that I healed them". Hos 11:3.

FAITH FOR VICTORIOUS LIVING

"But thanks be to God, which giveth us the victory through our Lord Jesus Christ". 1Co15:57.

"For whatsoever is born of God overcometh the world: and this is the victory that overcometh the world, even our faith". 1John 5:4.

Victory is God's plan and purpose for your life. Refuse to be a victim. You have what it takes through Christ Jesus to overcome every satanic force in the world. You were created to overcome and to rule all the powers of the air, the powers on the earth and the powers under the earth. The Christ in you is greater than the Satan out there. The faith that wins is in you. Walk in that authority and subdue every power of the wicked. Stir up the victorious power within you, and press on for your victorious lifestyle in Christ Jesus.

"The LORD shall cause thine enemies that rise up against thee to be smitten before thy face: they shall come out against thee one way, and flee before thee seven ways". De 28:7.

FAITH FOR YOUR OPEN DOORS

"I know thy works: behold, I have set before thee an open door, and no man can shut it: for thou hast a little strength, and hast kept my word, and hast not denied my name". Re 3:8.

Today in the name of Jesus Christ the Messiah, I agree with you for an unusual open door for a total turn around in your life.

Believe God today for:

- ❖ Divine ministerial open doors that will totally set you on a new ministerial platform in life.
- ❖ Stand by faith for divine marital healing and restoration.
- ❖ Supernatural connection to your God given life partner.
- ❖ Unusual financial open doors and financial growth.
- ❖ Divine open door and connection to your dreamed job.
- ❖ Divine business connections and Business opportunities.
- ❖ Believe God for changes in your immigration status.

❖ Open doors for unusual provision for your projects. "Behold, I will do a new thing; now it shall spring forth; shall ye not know it? I will even make a way in the wilderness and rivers in the desert". Isa 43:19.

FAITH FOR YOUR RESTORATION

"And I will restore to you the years that the locust hath eaten, the cankerworm, and the caterpillar, and the palmerworm, my great army which I sent among you". Joel 2:25.

"And David inquired of the LORD, saying, Shall I pursue after this troop? Shall I overtake them? And he answered him, Pursue: for thou shall surely overtake them, and without fail recover all". 1Sa 30:8.

"I will gather them that are sorrowful for the solemn assembly, who are of thee, to whom the reproach of it was a burden. Behold, at that time I will undo all that afflict thee: and I will save her that halteth, and gather her that was driven out; and I will get them praise and fame in every land where they have been put to shame. At that time will I bring you again, even in the time that I gather you: for I will make you a name and a praise among all people of the earth, when I turn back your captivity before your eyes, saith the LORD". Zep 3:18-20

FAITH FOR YOUR ESTABLISHMENT

"But the Lord is faithful, who shall stablish you, and keep you from evil". 2Th 3:3

"But the God of all grace, who hath called us unto his eternal glory by Christ Jesus, after that ye have suffered a while, make you perfect, stablish, strengthen and settle you". 1Pe5:10. "Now to him that is of power to stablish you according to my gospel, and the preaching of Jesus Christ, according to the revelation of the mystery, which was kept secret since the world began, but now is made manifest, and by the scriptures of the prophets, according to the commandment of the everlasting God, made known to nations for the obedience of faith: To God only wise, be glory through Jesus Christ for ever. Amen". Rom 16:25-27.

FAITH FOR A PEACEFUL LIFE

"The LORD will give strength unto his people; the LORD will bless his people with peace". Ps 29:11.

"Mark the perfect man, and behold the upright: for the end of that man is peace". Ps 37:37.

"Great peace have they which love thy law: and nothing shall offend them". Ps 119:165.

Peaceful life is possible as we put our trust in God, regardless of our circumstances. The peace of God is stronger than the pain we bear. Allow God's peace rule over your pain.

FAITH FOR THE DREAM OF YOUR LIFE

"The LORD hear thee in the day of trouble; the name of the God of Jacob defend thee; Send thee help from the sanctuary and strengthen thee out of Zion; Remember all thy offerings, and accept thy burnt sacrifice; Selah. Grant thee according to thine own heart, and fulfill all thy counsel. We will rejoice in thy salvation, and in the name of our God we will set up our banners: the LORD fulfill all thy petitions". Ps 2:1-4.

What is the dream of your life? What do you do for life? What do you live for? What is the meaning of your life as a Christian on earth? What divine assignment do you live to fulfill?

PRAYERFULLY CONSIDER THESE

- ➢ Noah lived to build the ark in order to preserve life on earth and to save his family.
- ➢ Abraham left his fatherland into the Promised Land in order to become the father of the people of God, the Israelites. He

loved God, had faith in God for a son even in old age and God did it according to his faith.
- ➢ Jacob wrestled with God for his blessing and he became the father of the twelve tribes of Israel.
- ➢ Joseph kept his moral uprightness even in a strange land like Egypt. He refused to be messed up with the sinful and immoral culture of Egypt and God raised him up from prison to the palace.
- ➢ Moses led the children of Israel out of Egypt, after four hundred and thirty years of captivity. He believed God, to cross the red sea and to go through the wilderness for forty long years through the miraculous working power of the LORD God. Joshua through faith in the Word of God, caused the River Jordan to flow upward, and they crossed the river through the miracle of God.
- ➢ Joshua with the children of Israel walked round the city of Jericho and through a shout on the seventh day; the great walls of Jericho fell down flat. Joshua believed God and commanded the sun to stand still and it did according to his word.
- ➢ Samson killed a thousand philistines with the jaw born of an ox. King
- ➢ David killed a lion and a bear and latter killed Goliath with a little stone and a sling. The list can never come to an end; the question today is: what will be written concerning your lifetime on earth?

My dear friend, never give up on your dream. Press on in faith until it comes to pass. Let me end here for the moment, I am scheduled to preach few minutes from now at the Living word charismatic ministry, Torino.

The Lord bless you.

PART TWO

Reign In Life

"What everyone wants from life is continuous and genuine happiness".

Baruch spinoza

REIGN IN LIFE

YOU WERE BORN TO REIGN IN LIFE
Your future is in your hand; for you to go to heaven is a choice, for you to go to hell is a choice. For you to be a blessing is a choice, for you to be a committed person is a choice. God created man with the power to choose and to decide, your choices and decisions determine the outcome of your life. Your future is a product of your will. God will not force you into anything.

You choose to do the things you do and the person you are is a result of the choices you make. Your future depends on what you decide today. The chief of a village in Africa called his children together after they graduated from primary school. He asked them to decide what career they wanted for their future. The first child said "daddy I want to continue my education, I want to go to a technical college". The second child said "I want to do sewing" and the third child decided to do carpentry in the neighborhood. Their father was wealthy and ready to do all that they decided for their future. And according to their decisions so he did to each of them. You need to know that today all these children have become the outcome of their choices. What you sow today will eventually determine your harvest tomorrow. Your decisions today will determine your life tomorrow.

Jabez created his future when he decided to change the course of things around him, he was born in pain but he decided not to end up in pain and sorrow, read 1 Chronicles 4:9-10. His faith in God and his specific request and desire, transformed his situation and he became more honorable than his brethren. Success and failures are the direct results of the steps we take. Right decisions leads to right ends and poor decisions will eventually lead to woeful ends. I want to call on you today to decide for a beautiful future and to take the right steps towards the dreams of your life. The Lord is waiting for you to take the right steps towards your God given destiny. For His thoughts for you are thoughts of peace and His desire is to give you a well planned end. If you don't plan to succeed you have planned to fail.

You were born to reign in life, go for it.

CHAPTER ONE

Breaking Satanic Ties

"As long as the mind is enslaved,
the body can never be free".

MARTIN LUTHER KING,
speech, Aug. 16, 1967

CHAPTER ONE
BREAKING SATANIC TIES

Satanic ties are legal grounds on which Satan and the evil forces bind people. They are like spiritual cables that connect people with the dark world. They are like legal documents that give the enemy full permission and authority to visit and to fulfill his desires on individuals, families, communities and even nations.

The devil is a wicked devil: but he deals with people that have connection and a relationship with him. The devil is the most intelligent diplomat; he is specialized in negotiations and persuasion. He walks with people that he is able to convince, he believes in dialog. He got Adam and Eve through dialog and negotiation. He got Judas Iscariot through dialog and negotiation; the dream to possess thirty pieces of silver became so strong in the heart of Judas that he had to accept to collaborate with the high priest to betray Jesus Christ his master.

It is the will of God that you willingly choose to do that which is right and pleasing to God; you need to have a good heart towards others. Give the devil no opportunity to have his will performed by you. Begin to break every form of satanic, evil ties in your personal and family life. Begin by faith to stand in the gap to intercede to break every satanic connection with your community.

The devil has never forced anybody for anything; he can never work without the will of man. The devil did not force Ben Laden and his agents to destroy the World trade centre. It was an act of his will, he collaborated with the devil and he became the cannel of destruction and death. No person will accuse the devil or hold the devil guilty on the Day of Judgment; for you do everything by your personal will. Let's examine some of the spiritual cables through which the enemy gets hold on people and generations.

SATANIC ALTARS

Satanic alters are structures, shrines, 'sacred places' etc, on which religious and spiritual rites are preformed or have been performed to other gods and evil spirits. {Read, Judges 6:25:26}. Gideon was raised up in a family situation whereby his parents dedicated their children to false gods and spirits. Altars were raise up in their compound to pay allegiance to evil spirits and the gods.

So many people believe in communicating with their dead ancestors. Many believe in gods, and they go about carrying the images of these deities. Some even invoke the spirits of their ancestors for assistance. Many today are direct victims to these satanic practices, physically and spiritually. For those who act as mediums between these spirits and the people seek to enslave the community with covenants and allegiance to the devil.

Today you need to be delivered from all forms of ties with satanic altars; for there is power in the name of Jesus Christ to set you free and to protect you from all forms of witchcraft and occult powers. These are some of the ways in which the enemy gets into partnership with individuals, families, communities and even with nations. I was born in an environment where every household had a god and children bore names of these gods. People carried their gods on them and the hope of the parents depended upon what ever the false prophets of these gods told them. What a bondage; we were subject to the spiritualists because of fear and desperation.

This is your season of deliverance. You were not created to be in bondage and fears; you were not created to live all your lifetime in manipulations and deception. Be free from the effects of ungodly practices in the name of Jesus Christ the only Son of God. The Lord told Gideon to cut down the altars that his father had erected and to build an altar in the proper manner unto the Lord. It is time to decide to separate yourself from your ancestral, personal or family altars. Put your entire trust and faith in the person of Jesus Christ, for He is the Lord of lords. This is your season to receive deliverance from all forms of bloodline curses and family strongholds gotten through ancestral family altars.

SOME OF THE REASONS FOR SATANIC ALTARS

Many people want to rely on something they can see and feel, thus the enemy provides false hope through false physical gods. Since they cannot see God the Creator; they turn to altars and man made images to represent their gods and they put their faith in them in search of spiritual virtues. Some raise satanic altars for personal or family protection and for protection of their property. Some as a means by which they communicate to their dead relatives; and others as a means to fight against evil spirits and to fight against their enemies. Some have altars as symbols and images for worship; and as a source of spiritual blessings for Prosperity and fruitfulness. Some build satanic altars as a means to gaining spiritual powers for influence in the community. Still many have personal altars for sacrifices to appease their gods for life, security, wisdom and authority. Some have altars as oracles, to consult for information and direction. Read: 1 Kings 11:4-11. King Solomon built so many altars for the gods of his foreign wives which became a snare in Israel and the kingdom was divided after his death.

This is a new season, a season of cleansing, and a season of rooting out all that the enemy has planted in our lives and communities; this is the season to disconnect in every way with the power of darkness. This is the time to rise up against all forms of satanic ties and break down all forms of satanic altars. This is the time to get rid of all that brings curses and backwardness in our communities.

Begin to clean the land beginning from your life and family. How many satanic altars did your ancestors erect for family security and prosperity? How many times have you been dedicated to the spirits of the dead for favor and achievement? You have to seek for total deliverance from the effects of satanic worship and dedication to evil spirits. Many of our ancestors practiced what is called libation; they offered money, drink and food offerings to the spirits.

These practices open direct communion and connection with evil spirits and all serve as ties with the devil and brings forth enslavement of many individuals, communities and generations. You have to totally separate yourself; denounce all connections with evil spirits and seek God for forgiveness. Be free from the effects of satanic altars in the name of Jesus Christ. "When the Son of God sets you free; you are freed indeed", Amen.

COVENANTS

A solemn agreement, promise, oath, treaty, or contract between one or more persons or parties. Covenants are agreement between two people or groups of persons that involves confessed promises and oaths on the part of each other. Covenants are sacred and binding and upheld with penalty for breaking.

TYPES OF COVENANTS

Covenants with God: Abraham, Isaac and Jacob had covenants with God. God is a covenant keeping God. He wants you to be in a covenant relationship with him.

Covenant with people: We have for example marriage covenants, blood pacts, service oath, Land covenants, peace treaties between nations etc. Remember the covenant Joshua made with the Gibeonites in Joshua Chapter 9, which became a snare to the nation of Israel, for they were deceived by the Giboenites. Don't engage in any covenant with any person blindly or influenced, covenants have severe implications.

Covenants with evil spirits: Many sorcerers, soothsayers, mediums and wizards lead people into covenants with evil spirits as means to receive answers to their problems and hidden information without informing their customers of the terms of the covenants. Many have been bound by satanic covenants because they were in search for wealth, health, children, security and power. Some because of the dream to gain influence and to stay in power turn to seek for aid from satanic priests and sorcerers.

Jesus Christ is the only way out, no matter the number of years you have been in spiritual bondage, Jesus is able and willing to help you and His will is to set you totally free. Confess to him as your Lord and Savior and denounce all forms of dealings with evil spirits: I break every form of satanic covenant in your life in the name of Jesus Christ. Amen. Every covenant you make does not just affect yourself but have lasting implications on your descendants. So many people are held bound by covenants they made with spirits of the dead. Some because of the desire to speak to their dead relatives end up being possessed and entangled by evil spirits. It is demonic to offer food, drinks and gifts to spirits; it is satanic to seek to talk to your dead friends or family members. Remember; they are dead and every thing people offer to the dead is offered directly to demon spirits. Read: 1Cor 10:20.

DANGERS OF COVENANT BREAKING

Read Lev 26:14-32. Moses enlisted fifty consequences for covenant breaking. Many are suffering as a result of infidelity to covenants they made. Many are today in unwanted conditions and undesirable situation because of ungodly parental covenants. God is the God of faithfulness; God requires commitment to our decisions. "Let your yes be yes and let your no be no". God condemns all forms of ungodly and demonic covenants and will hold all responsible who seek to trade with the devil. Remember nothing good can come out of the devil and all good and perfect gifts come from the Father above who sent his precious Son to give his life on the cross for our redemption.

The only way out is faith in the blood of Jesus Christ; the blood of Jesus Christ was shed for all our sins and there is power in the blood of Jesus. Denounce, renounce and separate your self by faith from the effects of your personal or parental satanic covenants.

EVIL AND UNGODLY FOUNDATIONS

Read: Ex. 20:5-6; Gal 6:6-10. Upon what foundation are you building on? Good and blessed foundation can guarantee a better future. A house with a wrong foundation is bound for future destruction. It is very important that you consciously lay a solid foundation for your future and children to build upon. Many are bound by spiritual satanic ties because of the foundation they are building upon, sin begets sin. Many are building their lives on a rebellious foundation. Some are building on bloodshed foundation.

As long as there is blood on your hands you will have to pay back, it's just a matter of time, and if not in your days your children will have to bear the cross on your behalf; except you seek for mercy and deliverance from Jesus Christ the Son of God. He died to pay the price for all our sins and wickedness. He did not come to condemn us but to provide a way out of all our bondages.

Today is the day of salvation; seek Him while it's time. Every head of state that gains power through bloodshed will eventually end up with bloodshed, the blood of the innocent souls they shed will cry out to God until vengeance and justice is awarded. Some begin their life with series of wickedness, abortions, and inhuman immoral arts, your only way out is true repentance and faith in the redemptive power of the blood of Jesus Christ. Through the blood of Jesus every form of sin and wickedness is atoned. For many years, many have lived a sinful and hypocritical live, their secret sins will some day be made public and the effects will be very painful.

SECRET SINS

They act as spiritual Satanic ties that binds people to a life of misfortunes, fright and oppression. Some are bound through witchcraft and occult foundation. Children that are raised up by witches and occultists have a tendency to grow with anger, hate and with an inclination to crimes. The children of divorced parents, lack parental love and care; they grow up with hate towards the father or the mother and because they are fed with false information from either of the parties they eventually confuse these children and create in them a vacuum and an unfulfilled lifestyle.

How did you get your wife or husband? Did you use tricks and lies? Let the Lord be the source of your blessings. Whatever the Lord gives will bring greater joy and lasting peace; whatever is gained How did you get your Children? Those who consult witch doctors and satanic priests for pregnancies open up their lives to evil spirits and no evil spirit can give a good gift. Seek the Lord for the fruit of the womb, seek medical attention and trust God.

God will surely answer and bless you indeed in due time. Whatever you receive from the devil comes with a dark future; what ever you receive from God comes with everlasting blessings. Halleluiah

How did you get the land on which you have built upon? What ever you seized from the poor will instead lead you into greater poverty and future troubles. For the Lord is the righteous judge and he will stand up for the sake of the poor. Bless the poor and God will continually bless you. How did you get your certificates? Did you work for what you have? Did God provide what you own?

You need to deal with all forms of ungodly and sinful foundations in your personal life and in your family life. The evil which you refuse to deal with now and on time will eventually deal with you on time. There is a need for true repentance and sincere cry for mercy, remember Ananias and Sapphira, read: Acts 5. Don't be like Ananias and Sapphira; they had no time to repent, but God has given you the grace to still have life today.

Drop this book down: go on your knees and seek God for forgiveness, confessing every secret dealings and sins in your life, tell everything to Jesus Christ. Secret sins and evil and ungodly foundations give birth to curses or misfortune in life if not dealt with.

Breaking satanic ties and deliverance from curses

"If my people, which are called by my name, shall humble themselves, and pray, and seek my face, and turn from their wicked ways; then will I hear from heaven, and will forgive their sin, and will heal their land". 2 Chronicles, 7:14

God has always provided a way out of every situation we may find ourselves into, all he wants from us is the willingness to cooperate with him for the solution. We need to humble ourselves to God from our hearts. Humility attracts God and brings to us God's grace and mercy. He wants each one of us to personally receive Jesus Christ His Son as our Lord and Savior. His word says; "as many as received Him he gave them the power to become the children of God". John 1:12.

Pray and take a radical decision from your heart to denounce all altars, covenants, evil foundations and confess all hidden sins.

"If we confess our sins He is faithful and just to forgive us and to cleanse us from all unrighteousness". 1 John 1:9.

Seek the face of God and seek his presence. He says, "And you will seek me and find me when you search for me with all your hearts, and I will be found of you says the Lord and I will bring you back from your captivity". Jeremiah, 29:13-14.

Through genuine repentance; that is totally turning away from all forms of wicked ways and totally yielding yourself to God and to the Word of God. These will open the door for you to receive the Holy Spirit in order to seal your life and to maintain your victory. Have faith for your total deliverance, put all your trust in Jesus Christ and feed on the Word of God for your total restoration. Through your faith in God spend good time with God in daily devotion and prayers, this will help you feed your spirit man with the presence of God and be renewed and continually refreshed day by day. If you are in keeping of occult items or materials from mediums you need to consult a pastor or any mature believer to help you destroy them and to pray with you.

Pray this prayer with me. "I break every form of satanic tie in my life and family in the mighty name of Jesus Christ, I set my live free from all forms of bloodline curses and family strongholds. I am free indeed in Jesus name".

CHAPTER TWO

Walking In Your Blessing

"The hardest arithmetic to master is that which enables us to count our blessings". Eric Hoffer

"All the blessings we enjoy are Divine deposits, committed to our trust on this condition, that they should be dispensed for the benefit of our neighbors ~John Calvin

CHAPTER TWO
WALKING IN YOUR BLESSING

There are so many people who have received Jesus Christ as their personal savior and are qualified for heaven but do lack the blessing of God to live on earth. They are heavenly good and earthly useless. Qualified for heaven but disqualified for earth. They are a burden to their family and the community; because of the lack of the Word of God and the covenant authority in Christ Jesus for their inheritance here on earth.

So many believers are saved but still walk in fear and are caged by the enemy of their Souls because they still walk in the flesh. Many are saved from sin but unable to deal with the crisis of life. So many people in Christ Jesus are still bound by the power of sickness and diseases. Born again, but bound with severe debts and failure in everything they do. This is not God's perfect plan for his children. His plan is total restoration of all that the first Adam lost through sin. His plan is to bring redemption from the power of sin and from the effects of sin.

Child of God you were born to be a prince with God; you were born to rule and to have dominion on earth and everlasting life with God in heaven. God wants you to live well on earth and worship him in truth and in Spirit. You are saved and anointed in order to sit with Christ in heavenly places in Christ Jesus far above all principalities and powers. Praise the Lord! You were born to be blessed and to reign in life with your Lord and Savoir Jesus Christ. Hallelujah.

GOD BLESSED ADAM AND EVE.

"And God blessed them, and God said unto them, be fruitful, and multiply, and replenish the earth, and subdue it: and have dominion over the fish of the sea, and over the fowl of the air, and over every living thing that moves upon the earth". Gen1:28. God's eternal purpose for Adam and Eve was to see them walking in the fullness of the blessing of the Lord. It was their choice to walk in the blessing or not to. God presented two options before them, to obey Him and reign in life or to disobey and be separated from the covenant blessings in the garden. It is God's desire to see his children fruitful in every area.

His will is for you to walk in your kingdom dominion and with every force of the enemy under your feet. You were born to subdue and to multiply abundantly. In the name of Jesus Christ, rise up from a life of defeat and oppression, rise up from a life of hopelessness and frustration, step into your blessing and authority.

Refuse to be trampled in life by the power of the enemy. You must decide to live as God intended for you to live, refuse to be anything less than God's best for you. Refuse that which society imposes on you; accept only your God-given identity. Your God is a great God; there must be the beauty of God on your life. Decide to walk in all the fullness of the goodness and favor of God. This is the season for the world to see the goodness and glory of God in your life. Your family should see that your God is a good God; your friends should see you and desire to follow your God. Decide to come out of the darkness of pain filled life and enter into the Holy Ghost filled life.

GOD BLESSED NOAH AND HIS SONS

And God blessed Noah and his sons, and said unto them, be fruitful, and multiply, and replenish the earth. And the fear of you and the dread of you shall be upon every beast of the earth, and upon every fowl of the air, upon all that moves upon the earth, and upon all the fishes of the sea; into your hand are they delivered. Child of God, all that was created was delivered into the hand of God's children." Genesis 9:1-2

Today man is afraid of the things that were supposed to be afraid of man. God's will is never to raise up cowards and victims, but to raise up sons and daughters full of glory and excellence. In God's divine plan man was supposed to be in subjection to no other power but to God the Almighty alone.

Today is your day of deliverance. Be delivered from the fear of man. Be delivered from the fear of evil spirits. Be free from the fear of the unknown future. Be free from the fear of loosing your job. Fear brings torments while faith brings healing and hope. This is the time to rise up in faith for all that is yours in Christ Jesus; there is a prophetic word that must be fulfilled in your life. I see you entering into a new season in your life; a season of praise and worship, a season of thanksgiving. Step by faith into your season of celebration. Amen.

GOD BLESSED ABRAHAM

"And the angel of the LORD called unto Abraham out of heaven the second time and said, by myself have I sworn, saith the LORD, for because thou hast done this thing and hast not withheld thy son, thine only son: That in blessing, I will bless thee, and in multiplying, I will multiply thy seed as the stars of the heaven, and as the sand which is upon the sea shore; and thy seed shall possess the gate of his enemies; And in thy seed shall all the nations of the earth be blessed; because thou hast obeyed my voice". Gen 22:15-18.

Abraham walked and lived in the blessing of God, in his days he was one of the greatest princes in the east; for God blessed him with everything. At the end of his life was richer than the beginning. His obedience to the Word of God led him into the fulfillment of all of God's covenant promises for his generation. Abraham is the father of the Middle East, without his natural seed on earth today, the economy of the world would crumble.

The seeds of Abraham control the oil price of the world. The same God that blessed Abraham has you and your family in mind. His goodness is not reserved only to some few individuals; his word says whosoever will believe all things are possible. You don't need to pay anything to God in order to walk in your blessing, all you need is to know what his word says about you and simple accept it and ask for it to manifest in your life. Praise Lord, this is a season of manifestation; let the blessing manifest in your life. Let his promise for you come to pass in Jesus name.

We all in Christ are the sons and daughters of Abraham and we have the promise of the same blessing as the natural seed of Abraham. Indeed we have much more greater privileges than Isaac and Jacob, we are called and blessed in Christ Jesus to \possess much more than just the physical but we are enriched with all spiritual blessings in heavenly places in Christ Jesus.

Today as the children of God we have the abiding presence of the Holy Spirit in us and God dwells in us and with us twenty four hours a day. My greatest blessing in Christ is the sweet presence of the Holy Spirit. He is my peace and my joy. I thank you heavenly Father for your goodness and mercy, that your love did find me and saved me, how can I ever say thank you enough. Through the Holy Spirit we receive the revelation of our covenant blessings in Christ. 'But God hath revealed them unto us by his Spirit: for the Spirit searches all things, yea, deep things of God. My prayer right now is for the good Lord to open your eyes to see all that is in store for you. You have more than enough. His will for you is a guaranteed future.

Today begin to thank and worship Him for the grace he gave to you that enabled you to discover divine secrets for your covenant blessing. Go in for all that is yours in God. Until the church is empowered spiritually and economically the spreading of the Gospel will be slowed down. You need to be blessed for the sake of the propagation of the Gospel. For what man knoweth the things of a man, save the spirit of man which is in him? Even so the things of God knoweth no man, but the Spirit of God.

"Now we have received not the spirit of the world but the spirit which is of God; that we might know the things that are freely given to us of God" 1 Corinthians 2:10-12.

Fill your mind with the blessedness of God and meditate on the manifold blessings of God, expect and believe for a season of unusual blessings and unexpected divine surprises, God want to surprise you with greater goodness and mercy. Child of God, begin to develop your faith for the uncommon blessings of God, expect the unusual and enlarge your faith for greater things. The goodness of God is much more greater than the human mind can ever imagine; enlarge your capacity to receive the abundance of God's overflowing goodness.

Don't only be testimony listener; become a giver of testimonies. That which God has done for others He can do much more for you. Rise up and begin to walk in the blessing of God for your life. The Blessing of God is what makes people different. Many on earth are struggling with their own effort, but we are different. The grace of God has done it all for us. The full price has been paid on Calvary for us. And by the virtue of the Holy Spirit, I pray that the blessing will rest upon you and make you a testimony on the earth.

SEVEN AREAS OF COVENANT BLESSINGS

Covenant blessing upon your hands and upon all that your hand touch. "For the LORD your God has blessed you in all the work of your hands; he knows your going through this great wilderness; these forty years the LORD your God has been with you; you have lacked nothing". Deuteronomy 2: 7

"Thou shall surely give him, and thine heart shall not be grieved when thou givest unto him: because that for this thing the LORD thy God shall bless thee in all thy works and in all that thou puttest thine hand unto". Deut 15:10.

Your hands are blessed by the Lord. Begin to confess and to declare to the hearing of the devil, that your hands are blessed by the

Lord and all that you lay your hands unto must prosper in the name of Jesus Christ. Declare that your hands are Anointed and sanctified. Declare that your hands must be productive and fruitful. Your hands are no more ordinary, for you shall lay hands on the sick and they shall recover in Jesus name.

Begin to lay hold on your covenant blessings upon your hands. From this day, nothing will die in your hands, nothing will fail in your hands, and nothing will be lost in your hands. Your hands will give unto many ministries that will affect change to many nations. Covenant blessing upon your mind.

"For God hath not given us the spirit of fear; but of power, and of love, and of a sound mind". 2 Timothy 1:7.

Sound mind is your covenant right in Jesus Christ.

Your mind is sanctified; your mind has been made completely whole by the blood of Jesus Christ our Savior.

Your mind is connected to the Spirit of God. Your mind is born anew and you will receive divine revelations because of your sound mind. From this day you will be a man or woman of divine inspiration and God will put into your mind kingdom secrets and kingdom formulas for divine breakthrough. Your mind was not made for stress and tensions, your mind was not made for confusion and restlessness. Your mind was not created for negative thoughts and fears. Sound mind is your covenant right in Jesus, possess your mind.

Fill your mind with purpose and vision; fill your mind with the thoughts of God's will. Begin to declare that your mind is completely sound; your mind is filled with covenant thinking. Your mind is filled with creative ideas. Begin to activate your covenant wisdom and understanding. Out of your mind will proceed productive ideas for nation. Begin to confess that out of your mind will proceed kingdom principles that will transform many nations and impact many generations. Let your mind be filled with the glory of God, Halleluiah. Think as God thinks about you. Covenant blessing upon your basket and on your store house.

"Blessed shall be thy basket and thy store". Deut 28:5

Your basket and your store must not be empty. Your pay slip and your bank account must not bring you sadness but should bring you gladness. It is God's will to fill your basket with all types of precious fruits. Begin to believe and to expect the blessings upon your baskets and confirm God's covenant on your store house.

This is what God blessed Joseph with:
"And of Joseph he said, blessed of the LORD be his land, for the precious things of heaven, for the dew and for the deep that coucheth beneath. And for the precious fruits brought forth by the sun and for the precious things put forth by the moon. And for the chief things of the ancient mountains and for the precious things of the lasting hills.

And for the precious things of the earth and fullness thereof and for the good will of him that dwelt in the bush: let the blessing come upon the head of Joseph and upon the top of the head of him that was separated from his brethren". Deuteronomy 33:13-16.

The Lord is a good God; his will is to fill your life with precious things. He wants to fill your basket with blessings and goodness. It is not his will for you to live an empty life; he wants you to be fruitful and productive. You were born to enjoy the fruit of your labor, from this day; you will never labor in vain, in the name of Jesus Christ. Covenant blessing upon your field.

"Blessed shalt thou be in the city and blessed shalt thou be in the field". Deut 28:3.

God's covenant blessing should be expressively experienced in your work place, in your business place and in your projects and investments. Your work and resources are part of God's provision in order for you to be fully equipped for the propagation of the Gospel. It is impossible to walk in the covenant blessings and be a failure in your job and business life. God's eternal desire is to see you His precious child excelling in your work place, strongly developing in your business life and succeeding in your investments and projects.

Begin to confess and to believe for the grace of God on your work place; believe God for His covenant blessing upon your investments and projects. The propagation of the Gospel of the Kingdom of God; the good news of salvation depends on the prosperity of the children of God, who will stand as sponsor and ministry partners for the advancement of the Gospel. Get hold of your covenants blessings, it is your covenant right for your fields to be blessed.

Your field is your source of income. Nothing should stop the flow of wealth into your life. I proclaim the grace of God, the Almighty on your field. The Lord's will is to see you rising up powerfully for his kingdom. It is the Lord's will to bless the source of your income for the sake of his glory. God is glorified in your prosperity and He is dishonored in your adversity. "I create the fruit of the lips; Peace, peace to him that is far off, and to him that is near, saith the LORD; and I will heal him", Isaiah 57:19.

"A man's belly shall be satisfied with the fruit of his mouth; and with the increase of his lips shall he be filled". Proverbs 18:20-21.

It is God's will to bless you with wisdom and to bless the words that proceed out of your mouth. Your lips must be fruitful and productive. "Thou shalt also decree a thing, and it shall be established unto thee: and the light shall shine upon thy ways". Job 22:28-29.

Words creates, words opens and closes the heavens, words heals hearts. Begin to speak forth the word of God. The greatest power in the universe is the power of the Word of God. God made all that do exist by His spoken Word. The Word of God in the mouth of the sons and daughters of God is as powerful as the Word of God from the mouth of God Himself. There is creative power in the Word of God. You create your world by believing and declaring what God has said concerning your life and future. Don't be influenced any more by your physical circumstances, don't be moved by your present situation, don't be perturbed by what people think and say concerning you.

Believe the Word of God for your life, accept and live by it. Let your mind and mouth be filled with scriptural confessions. Alleluia. It was the Word in the mouth of Prophet Ezekiel that transformed and created total new life to the shattered dry bones in the valley. Ezek37.

It was the Word of God in the mouth of Elijah that closed the heavens in the days of King Ahab for three and a half years, and it was by his words that the heavens were opened. It is the Word that heals; it is the word that brings life and restoration.

Speak to your situation, speak to your family, speak to your future, speak to your business; speak to your life, speak to the mountains that seem to surround your life. Your word has the power to root out and to plant, to kill and to make alive, to pull down and to build up. Speak out and root out all the mountains that surround your life. "You close your mouth, you close your future". Your future depends on what you believe in your heart and what you declare with your mouth; for with the mouth confession is made unto salvation. God is waiting for you to speak so that He can act. God wants to bless the words of your mouth. God wants to anoint the words of your mouth with life giving power. Change and heal your world by speaking peace, make a covenant with your mouth not to speak words that do not edify. Let the blessing of the Lord rest upon the words of your mouth, let your words bring great satisfaction and reward your life with goodness and grace.

Covenant blessing on your children.

"And he will love thee, and bless thee, and multiply thee: he will also bless the fruit of thy womb and the fruit of thy land, thy corn, and thy wine, and thine oil, the increase of thy kine, and the flocks of thy sheep, in the land which he sware unto thy fathers to give thee. Thou shalt be blessed above all people: there shall not be male or female barren among you, or among your cattle". Deuteronomy 7:13-14.

You are specially loved by the Lord and he who loves you does not desire to give you anything that will end up to be a hurt to your heart. His desire is to give you the best in live. He loves you and wants to see you blessed. He wants you to multiply greatly. He wants you to be blessed with all that makes life meaningful and pleasant. He has a special blessing promised for the fruits of your womb; all that will ever come out of you must be blessed and be peculiar.

Stand on the prophetic Word for your children. Refuse anything that is less than the perfect will of God for you and your descendant. Refuse failure for your children. Refuse pain and sickness. Refuse backwardness and all forms of retardations. Know that the fruit of your womb is blessed. Stand in faith for the salvation and establishment of your children and family. Begin to bless your children, prophecy concerning their future.

Lay hands on them and decree the will of God for their lives. Impart and fill their lives with the goodness and blessings of serving God. With God it is well and without Him all is lost. Tell your children that they are loved and blessed by God, Amen.

God's covenant blessing upon your Finances

"But thou shalt remember the LORD thy God: for it is he that giveth thee power to get wealth that he may establish his covenant which he sware unto thy fathers, as it is this day". Deut 8:18.

You were not born to be poor and wretched. You were born to reign in life for the glory and kingdom of God. God blessed Abraham in every area and
made a covenant with Abraham that his descendants shall possess the gates of their enemies and be great on earth.

"And the angel of the LORD called unto Abraham out of heaven the second time, and said, by myself have I sworn, saith the LORD, for because thou hast done this thing, and hast not withheld thy son, thine only son. That in blessing I will bless thee, and in multiplying I will multiply thy seed as the stars of the heaven, and as the sand which is upon the sea shore; and thy seed shall possess the gate of his enemies, and in thy seed shall all the nations of the earth be blessed; because thou hast obeyed my voice". Gen 22:15-18.

We are the seeds of Abraham through Christ Jesus and the covenant the Lord made with Abraham directly concerns and applies to us in Christ Jesus. The wealth of the nations belongs to the Lord, and we are heirs of the Father in Christ Jesus. Wealth belongs to the children of God, and the kingdom of God on earth can never prosper without the wealth of His children. Accept financial blessing for the end time evangelism. We need the financial blessings to reach nations with the Word of God. God is waiting for His children to step out for their financial inheritance; for the wealth of the nations will be transferred to the church for the end time harvest. Believe, accept and receive all that the Father has for you.

You were born to be admired and to be respected by all nations

Filled your mind with the beauty and splendor of the Lord; You are a prince and a princess in the kingdom of God and wealth and peace is your covenant rights in Christ. The psalmist rightly wrote that he has been young and now old but he has never seen the righteous forsaken nor his seed begging bread. The silver and the gold belongs to God for the prosperity of his kingdom on earth and He puts the wealth in the hands of his covenant children for covenant investments.

I live to fulfill God's purposes on earth; I am here to do only His will and his will is to invest to save souls. God is in need of covenant financial partners, people that will make a financial covenant with God. People that will be in partnership with God: to use the wealth he puts into their hands for the advancement of His kingdom on earth. Let the blessing of the Lord rest upon your finances in Jesus name; let the blessing of the Lord rest upon all your financial investments in Jesus name.

Receive wealth for God's Kingdom advancement

The Lord wants to fill your life with his beauty, value and glory. He wants you to be fully equipped to fully represent him on earth. He will bring beauty for ashes and garments of praise for mourning. You will be admired and respected in your community because you are called by the name of the Lord Most High. Praise Him.

CHAPTER THREE
Effective Spiritual Warfare For Your Inheritance

"The most persistent sound which reverberates through men's history is the beating of war drums". Arthur Koestler Janus "Pray as though everything depended on God. Work as though everything depended on you."

Saint Augustine

CHAPTER THREE
Effective Spiritual warfare For your Inheritance

There must be evidence of effective prayers and spiritual warfare. Prayer is not prayer until people see the evidence of praying. Let the world see the effects of your prayers. "Confess your faults one to another, and pray one for another, that ye may be healed. The effectual fervent prayer of a righteous man availeth much". James 5:16

Evidence is the result of effective prayers

Hannah will show you Samuel as the evidence of her prayers. Effective spiritual warfare should produce real evidence; there should be change in people and situations around you. Fruitful: Paul and Silas will tell you that their prayers were not in vain, they sang and prayed and the Angel of the Lord came down in the prison with an earth quake and they were miraculously set free. Acts16:25.

Effective prayers must be full of faith

Elijah will tell you that he is a man just like all of us, but he prayed by faith and the heavens were closed and he prayed by faith and the heavens were opened. Be a man of faith, be full of faith. Faith is the motor that leads us to unusual breakthroughs. Faith transforms negative situations and turns misfortunes unto great blessings. Be full of faith.

Effective prayers should result to an encounter with God

Effective prayers and spiritual warfare should cause men to meet God in a new and unusual way and also result to an encounter with God for total transformation. Our communities should have an encounter with God as a result of our prayers and spiritual warfare.

Effective prayers should be based upon covenant promises

It has to do with holding on the Word of God for divine visitation, breakthrough, transformation and testimonies.

Real prayers should result in changing people, changing lives and changing communities. There should be testimonies as a result of effective prayers. Prayers that do not bring forth genuine testimonies is empty talk and waste of energy. We pray because God answers. And God answers when we pray, Pray because God will answer.

Effective prayers should result in developing intimacy with God

Prayer should be prayed in partnership and intimate relationship with God. Prayers should bring oneness and develop intimacy with God, prayers draws us to God and causes us to wait on God and to remain in God.

Prayers should develop victorious people

Through prayers we have victory in life and victory over the forces of darkness. A man of effective prayers should be known by his victorious life. We win our battles of faith through prayers. The church that prays will be a church that wins; a nation that has no intercessors will be a nation in chaos and a nation ruled by occultists. Prayers breaks the powers of the enemy and opens the heavens for the release of the power and manifestation of the glory of God.

Effective prayers should produce tangible results

Effective prayers can be evaluated and should be evaluated. Praying without expecting results is a waste of time. The book of the Acts of the Apostles is full of evidence of effective prayers. Through prayers the dead were raised, through prayers sicknesses were healed, through prayers Gentile nations bowed to the Gospel of Salvation and through prayers many were filled with the Holy Spirit. Let your prayers be effective and produce results in Jesus name.

Ten things you should denounce in life through prayers

Death

Premature and untimely death is not your portion in Jesus name. You will live your full life span in Jesus name. I denounce untimely and premature death in your family in the name of Jesus Christ. Exo 23:26.

Defeat

"Greater is he that is in you than he that is in the world". Victory is your right in life. Hate all forms of defeat, for God hates defeat. His word says "they shall fight against you but shall not prevail against you". Jer1:19.

Destruction

No destruction or plague will not come near your dwelling; you are covered by the blood of Jesus. Read Ps 91.

Demotion

For promotion cometh neither from the east nor from the west, nor from the south. Ps 75:6.

You were born to reign, you were born to grow and be a blessing. Denounce all that seeks to pull you down in life. Take your steps upward and not downward, in Jesus name.

Depression

Peace and joy is your portion in life; let your heart be filled with singing and heavenly melody. Resist the lies of the devil about you and be filled with life again. Your heart was not made for sadness; decide to celebrate life in Jesus.

Deception

The devil is a liar, resist him and he will flee from you. Stand on the Word of God for your life. Only what God says matter in my life. Refuse to be deceived by any person or spirit. Be a man or woman of God's Word, be a man or woman of truth and integrity. Love the truth and hate all forms of falsehood. Seal your mind with the Spirit of truth. From this day you will never be a victim of satanic deception in the name of Jesus Christ. Seal your family from all forms of craftiness and deception.

Delay

There are so many people that good things don't come their way easily. There seem to be an unknown power that keeps them behind their age mates and colleagues. The Lord will hasten to perform His word in your life and in your days in Jesus' name. Refuse every form of setbacks in your life and business.

Disease:

For "by His stripes you were healed". Your body is the temple of the Holy Spirit and the power of infirmity has been broken in the name of Jesus Christ. Reject sickness and disease for Jesus Christ has paid a full price for the redemption of your body, soul and spirit. Be filled with the healing power of the Holy Spirit and keep your mind sound and free from all forms of fears and doubts.

Right now denounce all forms or sicknesses and receive your health in the name of Jesus Christ. Sin: Sin shall not have dominion over you; you were born to serve the living God in truth and holiness. Genuine repentance from sin brings favor with God and peace with man. Decide to keep your self from deceitful power of sin; for sins leads to death and hell. A life of sin leads to shame and painful living.

Stand in the power of the blood of Jesus Christ and keep your life from the power of the lusts of the things of the world. Enslavement: Many have made themselves slaves to the things they were created to rule; many are bound by various addictions and are bound by the power of darkness.

Today you can be free from every form of bondage. Wage war in prayers against the powers that have kept you from being all that you were born to be in life. Stand in your faith through prayers against the forces of darkness that seem to push you backward in life. Decide to live a victorious life; for the will of God for you is your breakthrough in life and to make heaven on the last day.

Stop wishing for change, wishes don't change things. Stand up for a new beginning in your life; you can make it in life. You have what it takes to be the best in life. You were born to reign in life, refuse to be trodden down by your circumstances and decide to stand up to create a new future for your life through your faith in Jesus Christ. Say after me: there is a great future ahead of me; nothing will stop me until I become all that I was born to be; in the mighty name of Jesus Christ.

You were born to win and to live a victorious life; victory is God's will for your lifetime. These are some areas you need to be in total victory. Victory over the world system: do not be conformed to the world system: remember you are a heavenly citizen living on earth temporally. Don't live like the people of this world, for they live by sight and are led by their sinful appetites and we live by faith and are led by the Spirit of God.

Victory over the flesh and sin

Sin is violating of the laws of God in order to satisfy our selfish, sinful desires. In Christ we are a new creation. Victory over temptations and trials of life: The storms of life are for a season; you will win as long as you stand by faith in the Lord Jesus Christ. You need to gain victory over evil influence, evil ideas and over evil thoughts. Your mind should be under the control of the Spirit of the Lord. Victory over emotional and Psychological problems: Bring into captivity the things that seek to bring you into captivity through the power of the blood of Jesus Christ.

Overcome your fears and pressures. The Lord is your peace and strength. Keep your mind save and sound. Victory over evil spirits : In Christ you have victory over Sorcerers, the occults, witches and wizards, etc. You were saved to sit with Christ in heavenly places, let no satanic or human wicked force oppress you any more. Exercise your victory over the spirits and gods of the land and over the effects of ancestral and family blood line.

Begin to pray for the breaking of satanic alters, breaking of ancestral covenants and curses in your family line. You need to gain victory over life's failures, limitations and close doors; decide for total victory today over addictions and uncontrolled temper. You need to walk in victory in your career. You need to stand up by faith for your breakthrough in gaining the employment you deserve and becoming the person you were born to be according to the scripture.

Believe God for financial victory; Victory over a lifestyle of debts and financial hardship. Believe God for Deliverance from financial stumbling blocks and misfortunes.

Trust God for total victory in your personal walk with God. It has to do with Spiritual prosperity and victorious Christian living. It has to do with intimacy with the Holy Spirit. I agree with you today for the prosperity of your spiritual life and I agree with you for spiritual growth in this season as never before in Jesus name.

Seek God for your ministerial victory: this has to do with ministerial breakthrough and growth. It has to do with achievement in your ministerial goals.

Decide for Marital victory: decide for your home to be a place or rest and refreshment and not a battle ground. Decide to bring order and control in your home. Seek to separate from every individual that wants to ruin your marriage and destroy your family.

"Behold, I give unto you power to tread on serpents and scorpions and over all the power of the enemy: and nothing shall by any means hurt you, notwithstanding in this rejoice not, that the spirits are subject unto you; but rather rejoice, because your names are written in heaven". Luke 10:19-20.

Command every knee, every negative force and every satanic influence seeking to destroy and hinder your life to bow today at the mention of the name of Jesus Christ. Begin to walk in your victory, it is time to stand up and fight, push back, resist, and rebuke every satanic resistance in the name of Jesus Christ. Push back all the negative powers of the enemy that seem to keep your family backward. Refuse to be ruled by failure. Refuse to be tormented by the power of hopelessness and despair.

Remember you were born to reign in life through Christ Jesus. Rise up in your heart for a new beginning. You can walk in total victory; believe in your victory through the finished work of Jesus Christ on Calvary. Talk victory; dream victory, fill your mind with victory and possess victory. Victory is your redemptive right in Jesus Christ. There is power in the name of Jesus for your total deliverance.

Deliverance deals with the following cases. Oppressions and depressions: Deliverance from emotional and psychological crisis, such as fears, uncontrollable lust, ill temper and addictions etc.

You need deliverance in three dimensions

Obsessions

This deals with deliverance from external forces that seek to gain control over your mind and soul. You need to resist ever negative and controlling voice that seeks to control and manipulate your life. Take charge over your mind in Jesus name.

Possessions

This deals with deliverance from indwelling spirits that have taken over the control of your will and life. A possessed individual is no more himself or herself. There is now a spiritual force directing and dictating the actions and decisions of the individual.

Initiations

This has to do with satanic and ungodly covenants. It is God's will to break every form of curse.

Deliverance from initiations has to do with destroying the effects of evil pronouncements and declarations.

It has to do with deliverance from the effects of negative bloodline.

It has to deal with breaking of satanic strongholds, soul ties and the destroying the addictions and the grip of sinful practices.

It has to deal with breaking of ungodly and family covenants, breaking of ancestral altars and breaking of ungodly foundations. Etc.

Deliverance has to do with people, places and even things. Every satanic and occult objects must be destroyed from your possession in the name of Jesus Christ. Cleansing and purifying of places and things such as; Idol worship centers, secret forests or groves, former serious crime centers and occult worship centers. Jesus is the way out of every form of satanic bondage. Read: Mark 16:9, 2 Cor 6:16-18, Mark 5:1-3,10, Gen 35:1-4.

Begin today by yielding to Jesus as your personal Lord and Savior and seek for God's Anointed servants to pray with you. "The prayer of a righteous man avails much" {I am available to answer your questions and be of any assistance, just send me a mail}

CHAPTER FOUR
Strategic Prayers

To be a Christian without prayer is no more possible than to be alive without breathing." Martin Luther King, Jr

CHAPTER FOUR
STRATEGIC PRAYERS

There is a need for you to know what to pray for and how to pray effectively. This chapter is a guide to assist you pray fervently and effectively.

VICTORY PRAYERS

"But thanks be to God, which giveth us the victory through our Lord Jesus Christ". 1COR15:57

"And the God of peace shall bruise Satan under your feet shortly. The grace of our Lord Jesus Christ be with you. Amen". Rom 16:20.

Decide today in the name of Jesus Christ to subdue everything that is not God's perfect will for your life. Through the blood of Jesus Christ, bring under your control all that seeks to dominate you negatively. Refuse to be enslaved by any form of satanic power in the name of Jesus Christ. Command every authority that seems to rise against your success and destiny to bow at the mention of the name of Jesus Christ. Declare your victory through the blood of Jesus Christ our Lord.

DELEVERANCE PRAYERS: since I have treated this in previous chapter I will just give you some reminder.

It has to do with:

Personal deliverance: Setting your life free from the life of bondage, infirmities and satanic control.

Family deliverance: This deals with breaking negative family strongholds. Denouncing ungodly family covenants, customs and idol worship. It has to do with breaking the power and effects of family witchcraft. Etc.

Community deliverance: This deals with setting communities free through the blood of Jesus Christ, from moral, spiritual and social decadence. Community deliverance has to do with redeeming the land from ungodliness and Satanism. It deals with overcoming the evil principality over the community for salvation, prosperity and the wellbeing of the community.

National deliverance: Deals with restoration of social justice, integrity and the fear of God. It has to deal with deliverance from corruption, false religions and occult practices. It has to do with deliverance from economic crisis and ungodly political leaders. Etc.

Today we root out everything, person, procedures and decisions that is not planted by the heavenly Father in families, in our communities and in our nations in the Name of Jesus Christ. Read: Matt 15:13, Jeri 1:10.

INHERITANCE PRAYERS
This deals with possessing your rightful possessions in Christ Jesus. It has to do with taking that which is your covenant right in Christ. Read: Gal 4:1-6. Activating and reaching out by faith to all of God's Promises and covenants concerning your life and generation. 1Cor 2:12, Oba 17, Deut 1:6-8, 2 Pet 1:3. Deut 1:21.
There is warfare involved in possessing all that God has promised us. The violent take it by force, you don't sit and wait for all that belongs to you; you have to arise and go for all that is your covenant blessings. Reach out for yourself, for your family and community. All of God's covenant promises and blessings are for those who will discover them, personalize them, and reach out by faith for them.

God has made a good will for you; seek to possess the will of God for your lifetime.

SALVATIONAL PRAYERS

"I say unto you, that likewise joy shall be in heaven over one sinner that repenteth, more than over ninety and nine just persons, which need no repentance".Luke Lk15:7.

"Likewise, I say unto you, there is joy in the presence of the angels of God over one sinner that repenteth". Lk 15:10

This deals with spiritual warfare for the souls and salvation of men and women. God is seeking for men and women with a burden for the salvation of lost souls. It includes; Individual salvation, family salvation, community salvation, national and Worldwide revival. Etc.

Will you stand in the gap for your family's salvation? Will you stand in the gap for your community? There is a need for congregational and personal fasting, all night prayers, prayer crusades, prayer walks, Spiritual mapping, and strategic salvational warfare and breakthrough prayers. Etc. May God raise up men and women with great burden for the salvation of others. Read: Jeri 62:1-7.

You can be the one to make a difference through your intercessory prayers. Begin today to spend just ten minutes or more a day to pray for souls. We need to see a great harvest of souls in these last days for the kingdom of God. Your prayers for revival has great effect in the nations, keep praying until the flood gates are opened and the Spirit of the Almighty God is poured out; keep praying no matter what you see happening around you.

RESTORATIONAL PRAYERS

This deals with recovering all stolen property. It deals with bringing back what the devil has stolen, and has to do with recovering all that was lost through ignorance and unbelief. It has to do with bringing back to life that which was dead. Bringing back the glory, gaining back your position and statues. It deals with restoration of your covenant blessings, your anointing, the Grace of God upon your life and your nation. It has to do with revival of spiritual gifts and fruitful ministries, divine favor, open heavens, restoration of all the years that the cankerworm and the locust have eaten, Joel 2:23-25. Jeri 33:6-7.

Restorational prayers have to do with seeking your missing and captured property. 1Sam 30:1-8. Etc. Your marriage can be restored, your job can be restored, and your children can be restored. Your finances can be restored, your church can be restored; the anointing you once had on your life can be restored and greatly increased. God want to restore His glory and power in His Church; He wants to restore heavenly authority to His ministers. God want to restore His glory and presence in your life today.

Refuse to be cheated by man or the devil anymore.

Refuse to be robbed of your privileges and blessings in Christ Jesus.

P-Pray

U-Until

S-Something

H-Happen

PROVIDENTIAL PRAYERS

Our God is *Jehovah Jireh*, Our provider. Phil 4:19. Ps 2:8. Luke 11:9-13.

There are things which no one can do for you or give to you, except God. Child of God, you must have faith for divine providence for your vision and for provision for your projects. Our God is the source of all good things. He wants us to recognize him as the source of all that we ever need for happiness and life. All that we need is in God; all that we have come from God. Your future, your success and your husband or wife; Your job, your happiness, your career, open doors, and divine security, your advancement and promotion in life, and every blessing in life is a gift from God. That is why we rely on God for without him no miracle is possible in our lives.

It will take divine provision for a genuine lifetime dream to be realized. Your faith in God should be much more for your future life than for your present life. Don't just live for today's pleasures, live for a legacy that transcends your generation. Positive history makers are men and women of faith in the God who does the impossible and provides a way where there seem to be no way. Believe the unusual and the uncommon, accept the impossible for your God can never be embarrassed by the magnitude of your request.

For you to reign in life you need the uncommon and the extravagant grace of God for the supernatural in your life. The God who provided for Abraham and for Elijah in impossible situations, that same God is your God. If we can do what Abraham did, we can experience what Abraham experienced. Abraham believed God, be a believer of every word of God and you will see the power of the God of the word working for you.

AUTHORITATIVE PRAYERS

"For verily I say unto you, That whosoever shall say unto this mountain, Be thou removed, and be thou cast into the sea; and shall not doubt in his heart, but shall believe that those things which he saith shall come to pass; he shall have whatsoever he saith". Mk 11:23.

Authoritative prayers deals with releasing the power of God within you, in the name of Jesus Christ, to challenge and to overcome the works and influence of the devil. Mk 16:17-18, Matt 16:19, Matt 17:20.

It has to do with giving commands to situations and people for positive change in other to establish the Kingdom of God and to enforce the will of God. It is written; "Thou shalt make thy prayers unto him, and he shall hear thee, and thou shalt pay thy vows. Thou shalt also decree a thing, and it shall be established unto thee: and the light shall shine upon thy ways. When men are cast down, then thou shalt say, there is lifting up; and he shall save the humble person". Job 22:27-28.

You have the choice to take authority over the circumstances you find yourself in right now. You have what it takes to gain control over all the storms of life and the waves that seem to sweep your feet off the ground. Take authority right now in the Almighty name of Jesus Christ and challenge the challenges that have challenged and crippled and frustrated your life for so long time.

You were created to reign in life, God's first words to man after creation were, "Be fruitful, and multiply, and replenish the earth, and subdue it: and have dominion over the fish of the sea, and over the fowl of the air, and over every living thing that moveth upon the earth" Gen 1:28.

Stand your grounds and face whatever may come your way with faith and courage. With Jesus you are more than a thousand of the enemy's forces. You have what it takes to win the fight; you have what it take to remain victorious in life. Authority is not for special people, it is in the name of Jesus Christ to all believers.

You were born to reign in life; the Holy Spirit's power is at your disposal. In Christ you are not an empty person the Son of God dwells within you. Take your rightful place in life and oppress every form of oppression, and challenge the challenges of your life in Jesus name.

COMMISIONING PRAYERS

This has to do with ministering in the office of an ambassador of Jesus Christ the Son of God, and speaking in the name and authority of Jesus.

It deals with giving of Charges, commands and commissioning. 1Tim4:14-16. Deut 34:9.

It has to do with giving of divine instructions. Jn 9:7, 2Kings5:10. Ex.14:15-16. 2 Sam 1:21.

Begin to command every authority, every negative situation and every unwanted condition to be transform and to align with the word of God for your life. Begin to commission creation to the purpose of promoting the kingdom of God. The 'mountains' are waiting to obey your command. "No assignment no performance", when you speak by faith; you cause God to give Angels tangible assignments to carry out on earth for the advancement of the Kingdom on earth.

PROPHETIC PRAYERS

It has to do with speaking out the mind of God to situations, and to the atmosphere for breakthrough and the revelation of the will of God.

It has to do with confessing and declaring the covenant word of God and declaring the Rheme word of God for your life, your health, your finances, your family and your marriage etc.

Begin to declare what the Bible says to your life, ministry, and your town and over your nation. Read Isaiah54:17. Isaiah 7:7. Ps 23, Ps 27. Ps 91. Eze 37:1-14. Dry bones shall rise again. Your miracle is possible. It is time to prophecy to yourself by speaking out biblical promises to your life in Jesus name.

Remember the Word of God in his mouth has the same effect as the Word of God in your mouth, the Word of God remains the Word of God; it must surely come to pass. The whole world is governed by prophecy. The future of the world is history before God and his people, because it has already been prophesied. We know according to scriptures what the future holds. Your future should no longer be a surprise because it has already been prophesied, walk into the revealed future. Stand for all that God has for you.

JUDGMENTAL PRAYERS

This deals with resisting, obstructing and coming against the will and agents of the devil. It has to do with destroying and frustrating the intentions and plans of the enemy. Ps 2:1-9, 1 Jn 3:8-9. Isa 7:1-7.

It deals with binding, rebuking and casting out demons and restricting the activities of the devil, Mk 16:17.

You are assigned to root out, pull down, destroy, and throw down all that the Father has not planted. Jer 1:10. Matt 15:13.

Judgmental prayers have to do with declaring spiritual warfare to dethrone principalities and controlling powers and forces of your land or your given territory.

Begin to destroy all the plans of the occults, spiritualists and sorcerers in your community. Every agent of the devil should never succeed in any given mission against the church and your community in the name of Jesus Christ.

Begin to render powerless all the activities of the wicked and spiritualists; Begin to uproot the powers of witches and wizards; dismiss, disarm and banish the powers of spiritual wickedness from your territory in the name of Jesus Christ. Declare your villages and towns free from the power and control of evil spirit. Let every knee bow before the feet of Jesus. Scatter the forces of evil and seal your community with the blood of Jesus Christ. Amen.

You are called to walk in total victory over all the kingdom of darkness. Jesus Christ is Lord of lords and King of kings. The gates of hell will never prevail against the children of God. Declare and pull down all satanic structures put in place to hinder and to deceive the children of God. You were born to reign in life through Christ Jesus. Reign and shine forth the glory of the Lord in your community.

CHAPTER FIVE

The Anointing For Successful Living

"A great leader's courage to fulfill his vision comes from passion, not position."

John Maxwell

"The greatest barrier to success is the fear of failure".

Sven Goran Eriksson quotes

CHAPTER FIVE
The Anointing For Successful Living

The anointing is what caused David to kill Goliath even though he was a shepherd boy and inexperienced in war. 1 Sam 17:50.

The secret was that Samuel had Anointed David and he was able to face the lion and the bear. From this day no devourer will stand before you in the name of Jesus Christ.

The anointing is what enabled king David to conquer all the enemies of Israel when he was king and to possess the land of Israel. Only by the anointing could David be able to possess the Land for Israel. By the Anointing of the Holy Spirit you will possess all that belongs to you and your community in Jesus name. The anointing is what caused Samson to kill 1000 Philistines with the jawbone of an ox. Judges 15:14-15.

From this day because of the anointing upon your life, all the enemies of your progress and destiny will bow before you in Jesus name. The anointing is what was upon Moses that caused him to be able to confront king Pharaoh, and to let the Jews go free out of the bondage of Egypt. It took the anointing to see the Red sea divide into two. The anointing will bring to an end your years of captivity and vain labor in Jesus name.

From this day you and your descendants will never be enslaved and oppressed again, because the anointing destroys the yoke. It was by the anointing upon Joshua that caused him to believe that walking round the walls of Jericho in obedience to God will cause the walls to fall down flat.

It was by the anointing that Joshua stood and commanded the Sun and the Moon to stand still; until he had gained total victory over his enemies. It was the anointing of the Holy Spirit that enabled Elijah to pray and caused fire to come down from heaven and consume his sacrifices, 1 Kings 18:36:38, the God that answers by fire, let him be your God.

Today the fire of the Holy Spirit will descend in a new and special way and all the temples of the false prophets, the occultist and all sorcerers will be on fire in Jesus name. It was by the anointing of the Holy Spirit that Daniel was able to know the King's forgotten dream and to give the interpretation thereof, Daniel 2:19. Today when the anointing will come upon you the mysteries of the Kingdom concerning your future and destiny will be made known to you in Jesus name.

You need the anointing of the Holy Spirit in order to live an effective and successful Christian life. He is the secret behind the success of all faithful ministers of God. Your success will depend on how much you will permit him to take hold of your life. Lord I pray today that you will pour out again the latter rain, let it rain upon the nations again, Lord. Let your servants be endued with an unusual unction of the Holy Spirit. Lord; let your Spirit fill your temple again. Lord I thank you for a new outpouring, by faith I can hear the sound of abundant rain.

The anointing is the secret of fruitfulness and abundance. The anointing of the Holy Spirit upon you will enable and facilitate your intimacy with God. Your salvation gives you the privilege of eternal life but your intimacy with God gives you the privilege of the abundant life. The abundant life is for all who will walk and live in the power and presence of the Spirit of God. The anointing takes away struggles. The anointing is the secret for victorious living. The Bible says in Acts 10:38, that Jesus Christ was anointed with the Holy Ghost and with Power and He went about doing good; for God was with Him. Jesus Christ could not do with out the Holy Spirit being upon Him, He relied upon the Holy Spirit. Luke 4:18. The anointing breaks the yoke. Isa 10:27. Jud 15:14

The anointing is the Constant abiding presence of the Holy Spirit, for supernatural ability and manifestation of God's power and glory. The Anointing of the Holy Spirit is what we need in order to be able to do effective spiritual warfare, no Anointing, no spiritual and supernatural breakthrough. No anointing no power of God in you, no anointing no supernatural wisdom and understanding, no Anointing no supernatural revelations and insight into the deep things of God. And no anointing no heavenly backing. Chickens without the hen are meat for the hawks; the Christian without the abiding presence of God is helpless before the enemy.

In all your getting, get the anointing of the Holy Spirit. Sickness cannot stand before the anointing; poverty cannot stay together with the anointing. Failures and defeat cannot share the same house with the anointing. Jesus told his disciples not to go anywhere or do anything; until they be endued with power from on high, Luke 24:49.

The anointing is Super Divine power in you, the anointing is divine wisdom; the anointing is divine understanding and the anointing is divine ability. Acts1:8.

The Bible says that when the disciples had prayed, the place was shaken where they were assembled together and they were all filled with the Holy Spirit. Acts 4:31

The Anointing is the supernatural coming to live in natural man; in order to make the natural man, God's divine instrument on the planet earth, in order to fulfill God's divine purposes. You cannot do without the Anointing of the Holy Spirit upon you. Zech 4:6.

For it is not by your natural ability but by the Spirit of the Lord. Elisha's dream was the Anointing, "I want the double portion of your anointing", and he got it.

Today by the anointing of the Holy Spirit, the unmovable will be moved; the ancient burdens and yokes must be broken. The crooked in your life will be made straight, the rough roads will be made smooth; the weak will be made strong and the dead will be made alive, when the anointing comes on you. The only thing that you need to get over dose is the anointing of the Holy Spirit. Be drunk with the new wine of the Holy Spirit. Go for the Holy Spirit today with all your heart.

SUCCESS LAWS

Success is not for special people. Nobody was born with a doctorate, nobody was born intellectual; nobody was born with success, anybody can succeed if they do what it takes to succeed. There are principles for successful living. Believe that you can succeed and become successful in life no matter what. You become what you believe, you work out to become what you believe you can achieve in life. You achieve what you work out to become in life. Success is not a gift; you work and walk unto success. Parents can give you inheritance but cannot give you success. You can be offered a good job but not success; you can be given a wife but not a good home. Nobody can give you success in life, you have to work for it and walk into it.

"Then Isaac sowed in that land, and received in the same year an hundredfold: and the LORD blessed him. And the man waxed great, and went forward, and grew until he became very great: For he had possession of flocks and possession of herds and great store of servants: and the Philistines envied him". Gen 26: 12-14.

Success loves those who love it and seek after it with all their hearts and trust in God. It will take dedication, commitment and trust in God to succeed in life. The things you love you attract and the things you despise you repel.

No success for lazy people, no success for idle people and no success for complainers. Success hates those who are in disorder and undisciplined in life. It takes order to succeed; it takes discipline to stay successful. Success walks unto those who believe that they can do better and become the best in life, and commit themselves to doing better and being better in every area of life. Success is the brother of purpose, pursuit and commitment. It takes commitment to the right purpose to succeed. I want to encourage you my special friend, to know that you were born to reign in life; you should never settle in anything less than God's best for your life. You can be much more better than you could ever imagine; there is a glorious future for you in Christ Jesus.

You were born to be light and not darkness.

You were born to be an heir and not a slave.

You were born to be God's special child, full of love and life.

Walk in the life and glory of the kingdom of God. Reign in life child of God.

You were born to succeed. Lift up your eyes above the present trials and hardship; your situation and condition will change when you change your thinking about yourself and trust in God for your next step.

You have what it takes to be successful in life before God and man.

Have a realizable dream

A God-given dream; a well defined purpose in life; something tangible, feasible and reasonable to put your all unto it until it be realized. Know what you want in life and go after it with all your life.

Do not be like Methuselah who lived almost a thousand years, and did nothing tangible with his life. Gen 5:27. He lived and died.

Abraham had a dream, for the Promised Land and for descendants. He gave up every other thing for the purpose of his calling.

Jacob's dream was for the Angel to bless him. He fought with the angel the whole night until he got what he wanted.

Joseph dreamed of greatness. He never gave up though through slavery and imprisonment, until he ruled the then world.

David had a dream to build God a house. He prepared all the necessary materials and handed them to his son Solomon to build the Temple of God.

Edison had a dream to produce electric light bulbs and he tried and failed so many times before he finally made it. No matter what it takes walk towards fulfilling your God given dream.

Be self disciplined
Be disciplined in your time management.
Be disciplined in your attitude and relationships.
Be disciplined in your financial management.
Be disciplined and committed to the development of your potentials and ability. Commit yourself in developing your God given gifts.
Be disciplined in choosing your lifetime career.
Be disciplined in your appetites and emotions.
Be disciplined in decision and promise making.
Discipline your mind. Get total control over fears, unbelief and distractions. Stay focused on your lifetime goals.
Discipline your mouth, speak that which is convenient, that which edifies and that which is profitable.
Have a strong zeal: be zealous in fulfilling your vision and purpose. 2 kings 10:16.
Be zealous towards your well-defined career in life.
Put action to your dream and vision.
Be committed to your commitments.
Be committed to your God given assignment.
Be committed to developing your spiritual life.
Be committed to your ministry and calling.
Be committed to your vision.
Be committed to the great commission.
Be dedication to your daily task. Pro 20:13a.
Be committed to your source of income.
Be committed to your obligations.
The church is in need of committed men and women; can you be one today. Have a strong desire to succeed. Hate failure and be determined to make it in life for the glory of God and in righteousness. 3John 1-2.

Have a heart, be bold

Face the trials and the challenges of life with courage and faith; you have what it takes to overcome all that may come your way. Refuse to fear; face your lion and your bear as David did. You will soon celebrate in life. Develop an unbeatable character; "Struck down but not destroyed". Read: Job 36:11-12, 2Cor 4:7-9, Jn16:33.

Seek to be productive and fruitful

Do not be a consumer, seek to be a producer. Seek to see good results in all you do. Seek to excel in life. Do not think you have already arrived but keep pressing on to the fullness of all that God has for you.

Prioritize your obligations

Most important things first: You can never do all things in one day. Do not die working without results. Know your strengths and weaknesses. Invest to develop your weaknesses into strengths. Develop your potentials. Constantly challenge yourself to grow. Attempt great things, have a heart for the uncommon things in life for God's kingdom.

Seek good health and a sound mind

This is your day for a miracle; failure is not your portion. You can make it, and you have to make it. Stand up for your destiny and breakthrough for your life. You must be sound mentally and physically.

Seek God's favor

God's favor is the grace that makes you distinct among men. God's favor is what qualifies the unqualified and the power that promotes the undeserved. Without his favor your labor and future is uncertain. Hold on to Jesus and abide in him, for without him you can do nothing.

THE SECRET

"I met God in the morning; when my day was at its best. And his presence came like sunrise with glory in my heart. All day long the presence lingered. All day long he stayed with me; and we sailed in perfect calmness over a very troubled sea. Other ships were blown and battered. Other ships were so distressed; but the winds that seemed to drive them, brought to us both peace and rest.

Then I thought of other mornings with a keen remorse of mind. When I too had loosed the mornings with his presence left behind. So I think I know the secret; learned from many a troubled way; you must seek him in the morning if you want him through the day".

Ralph Cushman

MY OLD BIBLE

"Though the covers be worn and the pages be torn; and some places bear traces of tears.

More precious than gold is this Book worn and old; that shatters and scatters my fears.

When I prayerfully look in this precious old Book, much pleasure and treasure I see; many tokens of love from a Father above, who is nearest and dearest to me. This Book is my guide, a friend at my side. It lightens and brightens my way. Each promise I find soothes and gladdens my mind as I read it and heed it today. To this Book I will cling, of its worth I will sing.

Though losses and crosses be mine; for I can not despair though surrounded by care, while possessing this Book so divine.

The Bible read it, love it and live with it. It is the secret of successful living".

Unknown

DIARY OF A BIBLE

January
A busy time for me, most of the family decided to read through the year.

They have kept me busy for the past weeks. Now they have forgotten me.

February
I was dusted yesterday and put in my place. My owner did use me a few minutes last week.

He had been in an argument and was looking up some references.

March
I had a busy day the first of the month. My owner was appointed leader of something and used me I got to go church for the first time this year,

Easter Sunday.

April
Grandpa visited us. He read me for an hour.

He seems to think more of me than he did when he was younger.

May
I have a few green stains on my pages. I am being used for public exams.

June
I look like a scrap book. They stuffed me full of newspaper clippings. One of the girls got married.

July
They put me in a suitcase today.
I guess we are off on a vacation.
I wish I could stay at home because I will have to stay in this thing for a month.

August
Still in the suitcase; no time for me.

September
Back home again and in my old place.
Have a lot of company too, "film and sports magazines are on top of me" my! I wish I could be used as they.

October
They used me a little today. One of them is very sick. Right now I am all shined up and in the center of the table; I think the pastor is coming to visit.

November
Back to my old place; I was looked through for some old papers today. One of the children picked me up and asked, "is this a scrap book?"

December
They are getting ready for Christmas, so I will soon be covered with packages and wrapping papers.

What have I done that you treat me this way?
What have I done that you refuse to love me?
Unknown

CHAPTER SIX
A New Season

Psalms 27

"In seed time learn, in harvest teach, in winter enjoy."

William Blake

"To be interested in the changing seasons is a happier state of mind than to be hopelessly in love with spring."
George Santayana

CHAPTER SIX
A New Season

Psalms 27

The Lord is my light

Your season of darkness is over.
Your season of insignificance is over, your light has come. Darkness hides, light reveals. Light makes manifest. The spiritual unseen satanic covering on your life is removed in the name of Jesus Christ. Light manifests that which darkness covers and hides. Your beauty must manifest, your potentials must manifest and it is time for your gifts to manifest.

Light shines and brightens; this is your season to shine forth.
I agree with you that: Your business must shine, your ministry must shine and your life on earth must shine with new grace and glory. This is your season to shine in every way and in every area in the name of the Lord.
You were born to be a light of the world; you have what it takes to shine. You have the Lord and his glory; let his glory shine upon you and through your life in a new way.

Let the divine light shine in your home and family. Every form of darkness and powers of darkness must be under your feet in Jesus name. The dispensation of the rule of darkness in your family is over; all that was covered by the power of darkness must be uncovered. Begin to drive out all that pertains to darkness from your family, drive it from your villages and towns and together let's drive out all that have any links with darkness from our nations in Jesus name.

The Light has come. This is your prophetic season to shine.

The Lord is my salvation

Your season of wholeness and complete soundness has come.

Your season of complete salvation, your season of total soundness and well being in every area has come. It's a choice to accept or reject; to receive it or doubt it. Believe and be saved. Wellbeing is God's will for you. Wholeness is your portion in life.

- ☐ Wholeness in your character.
- ☐ Wholeness in your mind.
- ☐ Wholeness in your body.
- ☐ Wholeness in your home, your marriage and family.
- ☐ Wholeness in your finances and job satisfaction.
- ☐ Wholeness in your heart and relationship with God and others.

Be made completely whole in every area of your life.

Your salvation has come; stress, oppression and depression have no more power over you; your deliverance has come.

The Lord is your salvation.

Confess this aloud: I am saved in every area in Jesus name.

What ever had kept you in pain and bondage has no more authority over you. Woman, your womb must be free in Jesus name; your womb must bear children and your enemy will be put to shame. You were not created to be barren; every power that binds your womb is broken in the mighty name of Jesus.

Your body has been crying for redemption because of the pain you presently go through. Declare your healing and deliverance in the name of Jesus Christ the Son of God. Reach out and receive complete salvation through the power of the precious blood of Jesus.

Confess aloud: My salvation has come and all that relates and belongs to me is saved and secured in the name of Jesus Christ.

Your season of fears and fright is over

Your season to walk in authority has come.

"And the God of peace shall bruise Satan under your feet shortly. The grace of our Lord Jesus Christ be with you. Amen". Rom 16:20

Begin to declare and confess aloud; I shall not be afraid of the lion or the bear; I shall not be afraid of the storms of life.

I shall not be afraid of the mountains or the valleys. I shall not be afraid of the sorcerers and the occult.

I shall not be afraid of the wicked or the witches and wizards.

I shall not fear by day or by night.

I shall not fear demons or Satan.

I will walk in divine authority.

In your neighborhood walk in authority; speak authoritatively, act with authority. In your home walk in divine authority; in your office work with divine authority in Jesus name. Your season of fear is over forever.

The Lord is the strength of my life

Your season of divine empowerment has come.

Power is your portion in Christ. Powerlessness is great frustration. His will is to be your strength and the source of your power. Today receive grace for spiritual power, economic power, moral power and intellectual power.

These are your covenant inheritance. Receive the strength of the Lord and walk in the fullness of his divine ability and grace. Weakness and failure is never God's will for you, you were born to reign in life, receive the supernatural presence of the Holy Spirit and be fortified in your inner man for the challenges of life.

Your season of total victory over the total enemy has come

The enemies of your life will stumble and fall. This is the season of the defeat of the enemies of your personality and destiny. The wicked will no longer prevail against your life and family.

Stop struggling with your enemies, the Lord has sent forth his Word concerning them, "they will stumble and fall".

Every dream killer will be broken down; every vision destroyer and inventors of confusion and false accusations will never prevail against the righteous in Jesus name, it is the Lord's battle. He will fight for you and you will only see them stumbling and falling. Rejoice your victory is sure.

Confess aloud: this is my season of total victory in Jesus name.

In this will I be confident

Your season of great peace and confidence has come.

Assurance and certainty in life is the result of absolute trust and reliance on the Lord. Confident living is your New Testament right, for Christ Jesus has paid a full price for all your lifetime on earth. The young shepherd boy David had absolute confidence in the Lord when he was faced with the challenge of Goliath.

The three Hebrew boys had great confidence that their God will deliver them from the furnace of King Nebuchadnezzar. You have no reason to be troubled and perplexed in life, the Lord will calm the storms of your life. Live a confident life. Declare aloud that it is well; stand in your faith, let nothing cause your heart to be moved. Peace is yours.

One thing have I desired of the Lord and that will I seek after:

Your season of definite purpose and specific achievements has come

What do you seek after? What is your reason for living? What is your innermost longing and burden for your lifetime? This is the time to prioritize your prayer needs; and seek God in prayers until it comes to pass. Many pray prayers, while God is waiting for them to pray a prayer.

Your Christian life begins with a prayer; your ministerial life begins with a prayer. Your future depends on one answered prayer that will revolutionize your whole life. There is a prayer you need to pray; is it a prayer of repentance? Is it a prayer of dedication? Is it a prayer of confession? Is it a prayer for direction? Be specific and purposeful in life. Know what you really want out of life.

Your season to see the beauty and glory of God has come

Moses prayed "Lord show me your glory" and God answered him. You were born not just to see but also to live in the glory and presence of God. Desire to see the glory of God in your lifetime. The glory has to do with the experience of the goodness of God and his special favor.

God is lavishing his unmerited grace and mercy in a special and uncommon way. May you see the beauty of the Lord in your days, May your personal life and family be filled with the glory of God.

Your season of total deliverance has come

The God you serve will not leave you desperate in the hand of the enemy; He always brings deliverance for his people. Whatever situation you may find yourself in today, does not define your future; Your God will come with his great and outstretched arm and He will save you. There is always a way out of every situation you may find your self. Jesus came on earth to give us access to the Father's throne of mercy that we may find grace and help in times of need.

Your season of divine uplifting and supernatural promotion has come

You were born to grow and to expand; this is a season of divine expansion and divine development. The Lord's desire is for his children to believe and to know that the blessing of God always comes along with uplifting and supernatural promotion.

He wants you to move forward and higher in life.

Promotion comes from the Lord. This is your season of promotion, accept it.

He wants to see you grow in the area of your calling. You should be making history for the kingdom of God. Covenant child of God, begin to walk in your covenant rights, to be the head and not the tail, to be a lender and not a borrower; to be a blessing to your family and community and not an additional burden to society. It is God's will to see his children in places of authority in the community. He wants to raise you up in order to raise others up. Begin to believe that you will occupy your God given place on earth.

Your season of supernatural harvest and answered prayers has come

Servant of God, hear the voice of God, you have sown seeds of love and compassion in the lives of many, your season of harvest has come; your labor will never be in vain. Many of you have sown seeds of prayers for many years, you have been praying and fasting for several key issues; you have been holding God for the salvation of your loved ones. The season for an unusual breakthrough and answers to your long term prayer requests has come.

Stop praying, start praising. Praise God for your harvest season has come; Praise God, for your years of trials have come to an end. Praise God for your season of favor has come. Stop complaining, start appreciating and change your attitude. Begin to celebrate the goodness of God and sing his praises.

Child of God; stop crying, your God will come with healing in His wings and he will wipe away all tears. Your trust will surely turn into testimonies, your weeping will surely end up with singing and dancing, and your loneliness will end up with great celebration.

The Lord has a Job for you, the Lord has a wife or husband for you; the good Lord has a blessing for your family. The goodness of God is not for special people; His grace is available to all. Turn your life to the Word of faith; trust every Word that He has spoken, He will surely fulfill His covenant promises. Only trust and fear not.

CHAPTER SEVEN

Productive Faith

"Success is the progressive realization of Worthwhile, predetermined, personal goals"

Paul J. Meyer

"Productivity is never an accident.
It is always the result of a commitment to excellence,
intelligent planning, and focused effort."
Paul J. Meyer quotes

CHAPTER SEVEN
PRODUCTIVE FAITH

"A pig was lamenting his lack of popularity. He complained to the cow that people were always talking about the cow's gentleness and kind eyes, whereas his name was used as an insult. The pig admitted that cows give milk and cream, but maintained that pigs gave more. "Why" the pig complained; "we pigs give bacon and ham and bristles; and people even pickle our feet. I don't see why you cows are esteemed so much more." The cows thought awhile and said gently. "Maybe it's because we cows give while we are still alive, but they have to kill you to get yours."

Unknown

You were called to be productive and effective in your faith and walk with God while you are still alive.

The following is an account generally given on how the apostles died. They all died in active and productive service to God. Your faith should produce lasting fruits and results.

- ➢ Matthew: He was slain with a sword in Ethiopia.
- ➢ James the son of Zebedee: beheaded at Jerusalem by Herod.
- ➢ James the brother of the Lord: thrown from the pinnacle of the temple and then killed with a club.
- ➢ Philip: hanged against a pillar at Hieropolis, a City of Phrygia.
- ➢ Bartholomew: Flayed alive at Albahapolis, in Armenia.
- ➢ Andrew: martyred on the cross at Patre, in Achaia.
- ➢ Thomas: killed with a lance at Coromanded, in East Indies.
- ➢ Thaddeus: shot to death with arrows.

- Simon Zelotes: crucified in Persia.
- Simon Peter: crucified, head downward.
- Matthias: stoned, then beheaded.
- Judas: hanged himself.
- John: died a natural death.
- Paul: beheaded at Rome.

My dear Christian friend, Christianity and the salvation of the nations is founded upon the sacrificial blood of the lamb and on the blood of the faithful followers, who died for the witness of the resurrection and Lordship of the Jesus Christ: what will your faith in Christ accomplish for your God in your generation?

In the days of the early church they had no Christian literatures, the Apostles had no Radio or TV stations and no telephone communications to facilitate their task, yet they did exploits for God and brought about great transformation that has affected the whole world. Your faith can yield great results for the kingdom. Your faith can bring great transformation in the lives of many. The nations are waiting for the manifestation of the sons of God.

Begin to belief and to confess that you can do great things and will do great things for the Kingdom of God through Christ Jesus.

Let us examine Mark chapter two; faith has the power to give birth to a brand new future.

Read Mark. 2:1-12. "And again he entered into Capernaum after some days; and it was noised that he was in the house. And straightway many were gathered together, insomuch that there was no room to receive them, no, not so much as about the door: and he preached the word unto them. And they come unto him, bringing one sick of the palsy, which was borne of four. And when they could not come nigh unto him for the press, they uncovered the roof where he was: and when they had broken it up, they let down the bed wherein the sick of the palsy lay. When Jesus saw their faith, he said unto the sick of the palsy, Son, thy sins be forgiven thee. But there were certain of the scribes sitting there, and reasoning in their hearts, why doth this man thus speak blasphemies? Who can forgive sins but God only?

And immediately when Jesus perceived in his spirit that they so reasoned within themselves, he said unto them, why reason ye these things in your hearts?

Whether is it easier to say to the sick of the palsy, Thy sins be forgiven thee; or to say, Arise, and take up thy bed, and walk? But that ye may know that the Son of man hath power on earth to forgive sins, he saith to the sick of the palsy, I say unto thee, Arise, and take up thy bed, and go thy way into thine house. And immediately he arose, took up the bed, and went forth before them all; insomuch that they were all amazed and glorified God, saying, we never saw it on this fashion". KJV

Read these verses carefully again and let us examine the five categories of persons involved in this particular passage. It is the will of our Father in heaven to see us his children, in victory and celebrating life. Your faith must be fruitful and productive. Your faith must bring forth tangible results and testimonies.

Five categories of people in this occasion
1. Those that were standing around Jesus and about the door.

They had no determination for anything; some came just to admire and to listen to something new from Jesus. I call them the spectators. They came empty and returned empty. They have no purpose for life. There was no longing for anything that could cause them to press onto Jesus for something tangible. There are many today who are in he house of God, others attend Gospel crusades and just look and watch the events taking place. Child of God, stop watching; move forward and press on for a personal breakthrough. You were born to reign in life, stop being a spectator, press on by faith.

2. The four men who carried their friend and sent him through the roof to see Jesus.

These are those who assist others to come to Jesus and to get their breakthrough but they themselves never meet Jesus or have any personal encounter with him. I call them the church workers. They usher people to Jesus but they never see Jesus. They usher people to receive their miracles but they go home the same. They are like some intercessors who pray for the deliverance of others but they themselves go home oppressed, distressed and sick.

Don't work for God without God in you.

3. The scribes, who came to find faults; Vs 6.

They had no positive contributions to make but to find out what had not been done rightly. I call them backsliders. Stop living to find faults in the lives and ministries of other. Seek to build and not to tear down.

Do something for yourself and for your God. You will never be perfect, do what you can do and do the best that you can ever do for the glory of God.

Don't live to be a faultfinder with the ministry of criticism and condemnation. Never believe that you alone have the truth and all who don't do things your way are all wrong and not spiritual. Don't seek to split people seek to unite people. Be a blessing and not the cause of the failures and pain in the lives of other people. You are called to give your own godly contribution to make the world a better place and the church a more glorious family.

4. The paralyzed man who received his miracle; Vs 11.

He experienced the power of God and had a personal encounter with Jesus. I call him the believer. He came in sick but went home totally healed; he came in being carried but he went back home by himself. He came paralyzed but went back home walking and carrying his bed. He came desperate but went back home celebrating. Alleluia. Be a believer, be a partaker of the grace of God. Let your faith produce results. Let your faith cause you to rejoice and be glad in Christ. Let your faith have tangible effects and bring effective changes in your life and community.

5. Those who glorified God because of the testimony of the paralyzed man

They glorified God because of what they saw Jesus did in the life of their friend. I call them the observers and the storytellers. They never have anything to testify of what God did in their own lives. They are specialized in story telling, they are professional reporters. You need to believe for a personal encounter with Jesus; you need a first hand face to face meeting with Jesus for yourself. You need Jesus to touch you at the point of your need.

Believe for a total transformation and a season of revolution in your life and ministry.

Don't be an observer be a partaker of the power of God for your miracle.

Don't be a spectator in life: Be a partaker of every blessing of faith in Jesus.

Don't just be busy body church worker: be a recipient of the grace of God for your every need in life.

Don't be a faultfinder and a backslider: be a man and a woman of faith.

Don't be an observer and a storyteller: be a believer; believe God for the impossible, believe the Word of God; have faith in the God of miracles, signs and wonders.

Jesus Christ has not changed; make up your mind to know him personally and to experience his wonder working power for yourself and then to reach others with the testimony of what he has done for you. The God we serve want to fill your life with testimonies, He wants to be glorified in your life. His joy is to see his children happy and blessed, that is why He sent His only Son to die on the cross for our salvation.

Make heaven glad through your faith.

Benefits of faith

Men of faith will provoke divine encounters with God for total transformation and breakthrough.

Men of faith will always have personal testimonies.

Men of faith will experience God in their situation in a personal way.

Men of faith will Come with burdens and return with blessings.

Men of faith will come sick and return totally healed.

Men of faith will not just see what God has done for others but will be partakers of every covenant blessing in Christ.

Men of faith will see Jesus in action in their lives.

Men of faith will have abundance when others are dying of lack.

Men of Faith will rejoice while others are crying and complaining.

Men of faith will always have hope while others are desolate.

Men of faith will be saved and raptured at the coming of Jesus Christ, while others go through unbearable conditions.

Men and women of faith have a place in heaven.

Be a man of faith; do not let your faith in God be in vain, your faith should produce tangible results.

Let your family enjoy the fruit of your faith in God.

Let your community partake of the benefits of your prayers of faith.

Men of faith will see possibilities when everybody else sees impossibilities.

Men of faith will go through the waters and the fire unharmed.

Men of faith don't wish for things to change; they cause things to change.

Men of faith are not complainers; they are 'proclaimers'; they proclaim the Word of God and the love of God.

Men of faith are not sympathizers; they are world changers, through the declaration of the Word of faith.

Men of faith are not extra ordinary people; they are men who chose to believe every Word of God.

Daniel spent a weekend in the lion's den unharmed, because he was a man of faith. Meshach, Shadrach and will Abednego went through king Nebuchadnezzar's burning fiery furnace unharmed; for the flames had no power over them, because they were men of faith. Be a man and woman of faith and not of fear and doubts. Lay down your human way of thinking and reasoning; fill your mind with the Word of God and the faith of God. Be a believer; choose to believe than to doubt.

CHAPTER EIGHT

Greater Grace

"Grace isn't a little prayer you chant before receiving a meal. It's a way to live"

Jackie Windspear

"Beauty without grace is the hook without the bait."
Ralph Waldo Emerson

CHAPTER EIGHT
GREATER GRACE

Don't find fault with the man who limps, or stumbles along the road; unless you have worn the shoes that he wears, or struggled beneath the burdens that he bears.

Don't sneer at the man who's down today, unless you have felt the blow that caused his fall; or felt the shame that only the fallen know.

The grace of God is what makes a difference in people. The grace qualifies the unqualified, the grace gives strength to the fainting hearted; the grace gives wisdom to the simple and success to the despised and rejected.

Hard work without the grace of God results to greater frustration, for it is God who gives the increase.

There are many degree holders who are jobless, there are many intelligent people who are helpless; there are many rich people who are desperate and there are many hard working people who are very poor; because success comes from God through His grace.

Parents may give you an inheritance, but can never give you success. A school may give you certificates but cannot guarantee your success in life.

You may invest in a promising project, you may invest in a business that seems so lucrative but your success will only be by the grace of God. One disaster can crumble and cripple all your dreams and cause you to become what you never dreamed of. For only by grace are we saved through faith. Let the grace of God change the story of your life.

Biblical surprises

- Satan never believed that God would one day cast him out of heaven; he never believed that he would one day loose his place and position among the angels of God.
- Adam never believed that one day God would cast him out of his presence and out of the Garden of Eden.
- Cain never dreamed that he would one day be a murderer and a fugitive on the face of the earth.
- Noah never dreamed that he would one day be the only man on earth with his family, until it came to pass.
- Jacob never believed that his children would become slaves in Egypt for four hundred years
- Joseph never believed that one day he would be a slave in a foreign land and that his own brothers would sell him.
- Moses never dreamt that he would one day run away from Egypt and become a servant to a Midianite. For forty years he was a shepherd, from the palace to wandering on the mountains with Jethro's sheep; working without any income.
- Moses never believed that King Pharaoh would one day bow to him and that he would be the one to bring deliverance to the Jews from four hundred years of slavery.
- Joshua the servant of Moses never dreamt that he would be chosen by God to replace Moses. From a common servant to the Nation's main leader with the assignment of taking them into the Promised Land.
- David the shepherd son of Jesse never could think that he would become the king of Israel; and that he would be the 'Father' of Jesus the Messiah. For he had no place of recognition even in his father's house.
- Jonah the prophet to Nineveh was so much surprised by the repentance of the people of Nineveh, for he knew that they were so wicked, that they could not turn to God. You know, he was so much offended with their repentance.

- The Apostles were so much in a great surprise, when Jesus was finally arrested and crucified. Though He had foretold them concerning His death. Yet they all thought it was a dream; and His resurrection was a greater surprise to them than His death.
- For Saul to become a follower of Jesus and later become an Apostle was a greater surprise to Paul himself and the Sanhedrin council in Jerusalem. He was transformed from an antichrist to an Apostle of Christ overnight. Halleluiah.
- How could anyone ever believe that Peter the common fisherman could become so powerful and influential, in a way that the whole nation of Israel could not withstand his wisdom and authority.
- Who could ever believe that a simple boy born in a village so remote in West Africa could ever become a channel of blessing to the nations? My entire life is the result of the grace of God.
- The grace comes with even more greater surprises.

The grace comes with uncommon favor and uncommon unction for uncommon achievements.

This is your season for greater grace. Your future will be a great surprise to your enemies.

"And with great power gave the apostles witness of the resurrection of the Lord Jesus: and great grace was upon them all. Neither was there any among them that lacked: for as many as were possessors of lands or houses sold them, and brought the prices of the things that were sold". Acts 4:33-34

THE MYSTERIES OF GRACE

Grace is unmerited

"For by grace are ye saved through faith; and that not of yourselves: it is the gift of God". Eph 2:8.

But Noah found grace in the eyes of the LORD, Gen 6:8.

Behold now, thy servant hath found grace in thy sight, and thou hast magnified thy mercy, which thou hast showed unto me in saving my life; and I cannot escape to the mountain, lest some evil take me, and I die. Gen 19:19:

Grace is obtainable

"And the king loved Esther above all the women, and she obtained grace and favor in his sight more than all the virgins; so that he set the royal crown upon her head, and made her queen instead of Vashti", Es 2:17.

"And it was so, when the king saw Esther the queen standing in the court, that she obtained favor in his sight: and the king held out to Esther the golden scepter that was in his hand. So Esther drew near, and touched the top of the scepter". Est. 5:2

Let us therefore come boldly unto the throne of grace that we may obtain mercy, and find grace to help in time of need, Heb 4:16.

Grace can be given and can be withheld

"For the LORD God is a sun and shield: the LORD will give grace and glory: no good thing will he withhold from them that walk uprightly". Ps 84:11.

"Likewise, ye younger, submit yourselves unto the elder. Yea, all of you be subject one to another, and be clothed with humility: for God resisteth the proud, and giveth grace to the humble". 1Pe 5:5.

"Surely he scorneth the scorners: but he giveth grace unto the lowly". Pr 3:34.

Grace can be received or rejected.

"And of his fullness have all we received, and grace for grace". John 1:16.

"For if by one man's offence death reigned by one; much more they which receive abundance of grace and of the gift of righteousness shall reign in life by one, Jesus Christ" Ro 5:17.

Grace can be developed

"But grow in grace, and in the knowledge of our Lord and Savior Jesus Christ. To him be glory both now and forever, Amen". 2 Pet 3:18.

"Grace and peace be multiplied unto you through the knowledge of God and of Jesus our Lord". 2 Pet 1:2.

Grace can be abused

"For there are certain men crept in unawares, who were before of old ordained to this condemnation, ungodly men, turning the grace of our God into lasciviousness, and denying the only Lord God and our Lord Jesus Christ" Jude 1:4.

Grace can be Unction or a possession

"Wherefore we receiving a kingdom which cannot be moved, let us have grace, whereby we may serve God acceptably with reverence and godly fear" Heb 12:28.

Grace is in measures

"But he giveth more grace. Wherefore he saith, God resisteth the proud, but giveth grace unto the humble" Jas 4:6.

"For I say, through the grace given unto me to every man that is among you, not to think of himself more highly than he ought to think; but to think soberly, according as God hath dealt to every man the measure of faith". Rom 12: 3.

"Having then gifts differing according to the grace that is given to us, whether prophecy, let us prophesy according to the proportion of faith" Rom 12:6.

Grace can be a benediction

The grace of our Lord Jesus Christ be with you all; Amen, Rev 22:21.

Grace is a spirit

"And I will pour upon the house of David and upon the inhabitants of Jerusalem, the spirit of grace and of supplications: and they shall look upon me whom they have pierced and they shall mourn for him, as one mourneth for his only son and shall be in bitterness for him, as one that is in bitterness for his firstborn". Zech 12:10.

Seek God for his manifold grace upon your life. When God qualifies you no man can ever disqualify you. When God appoints you no man can disapprove you. You need the grace of God, for without him we can do nothing as we ought to.

CHAPTER NINE
Vision And Purpose

"Vision looks inward and becomes duty.
Vision looks outward and becomes aspiration.
Vision looks upward and becomes faith".
Stephen S

"Vision without action is a daydream.
Action without vision is a nightmare"
Japanese Proverb

CHAPTER NINE
VISION AND PURPOSE

Men and women of purpose have a standard life style; they have life principles on which they build upon. It is impossible to be a lazy person and expect to prosperous. It is impossible to be become unorganized and in disorder and be an achiever on earth. Vision and purpose goes alone with great responsibility. A man with clear purpose in life; should be a man with a solid moral character.

How would you behave if Jesus came to your home.

"If Jesus came to your house to spend a day or two; if He came unexpectedly, I wonder what you will do. I know you will give your nicest room: to such an honored guest. All the food you'd serve to Him would be the best.

And you would keep assuring him you're glad to have him there...., that serving Him in your own home is joy beyond compare. But when you saw him coming, would you meet him at the door with arms outstretched in welcome to your heavenly visitor? Or would you have to change your clothes before you let him in: or hide some magazines and some films and then put the Bible where they'd been?

Would you turn off your TV and hope He hadn't heard and wished you hadn't uttered that last, loud, hasty, nasty, abusive word?

Would you hide your worldly music and put some hymnbooks out? Could you let Jesus walk right in, or would you rush about.

And I wonder if the Savior spent a day or two with you, would you go right on doing the things you always do? Would you keep right saying the things you always say? Would life for you continue as it does from day to day? Would your family conversation keep up its usual pace and would you find it hard each meal to say a table grace? Would you sing the songs you always sing and read the books you read and let him know the things on which your mind and spirit feed on?

Would you take Jesus with you everywhere you'd planned to go, or would you maybe change your plans for just a day or so? Would you be glad to have him meet your closest friends or would you hope they'd stay away until His visit ends?

Would you be glad to have him stay forever on and on, or would you sigh with great relief when He at last was gone"?

Unknown

It might be interesting to know the things that you would do if Jesus Christ in person came to spend some time with you. Be a man of honest character, be a trust worthy person. Be a man dedicated to fulfilling a lifetime dream. Be a man with a constant focus on the goals and purposes of your life.

Let your vision and lifetime purposes create in you a character of integrity and discipline.

Let your dreams develop in you the spirit of excellence and steadfastness. Poor character is the main cause of lack of success and greater achievements in life. If you cannot manage your life, how can you manage a project successfully? How can you manage other staff and how can you manage money properly?

Meditate on these

- ➢ The most destructive habit is worry. To be a man of purpose you need to overcome worries and focus on your vision without fears and doubts.
- ➢ The greatest joy is in giving. The seeds you sow they live forever, the seeds you eat they die forever. Don't be a stingy person; God blesses the generous.

- The greatest loss is a soul lost in hell. Let your vision and purpose affect the lives of people and cause them to live for heaven. For what shall it profit a man, if he gains the world and losses his soul?
- The most satisfying work is to help others. Don't live just for yourself, live for others. Seek the joy and peace of others.
- The ugliest personality trait is selfishness. God will always bless those who seek to be a blessing. God will always provide to channels of blessings.
- The most endangered species is dedicated leaders. Today they are many professional leaders who have no heart for the well being of their people, because they are not dedicated to God or to their post of duty.
- Our greatest natural resource is our youths. If we neglect them they will be deformed by the world. They need adequate information, training and counseling. In other to create in them the right perspectives for life. For wrong vision produces terrorist and confused citizens.
- The greatest "short in the arm" is encouragement. Every body can do better if he or she is encouraged. Be an encourager and be a motivator.
- The greatest problem to overcome is fear. Fear builds false and nonexistent images in the minds of people. Fear is the greatest enemy of your future. Walk by faith and not by fear; cause your fears to fear you.
- The most effective sleeping pill is peace of mind; and the only doctor who offers it is Jesus. Real people must believe in the real person and the real person is Jesus Christ, the only prescription for real peace of mind.
- The most crippling failure disease is excuses and the bondage of procrastination. Do what you have to do and start to do it now. What you do with your time now will determine how your tomorrow will look like.

- The most powerful force in life is the force of love. The force of love caused God to send His only Son from heaven to earth just to die for me and for you. Have you received His son Jesus Christ into your heart as your personal savior? If not; do it right away, ask Him to come into your heart and be your Lord and savior.
- The most dangerous practice is gossip. Gossip is born out of jealousy and hypocrisy.
- The world's most incredible computer is the brain. Be careful with what you use your brain to do. Make the right use of your brain. Use your brain to build and not to destroy.
- The worst thing in life is to be without hope. Hopelessness is the mother of crimes and wickedness. Jesus is the source of true hope and assurance in life.
- The deadliest weapon on earth is the tongue. Wrong words give birth to strife; strife gives birth to evil plans and evil plans give birth to destructions. Wars are born by proud and evil words. Don't kill by what you say; Speak peace and create peace and harmony.
- The two most power filled words are "I can". God has put all that you need in you. Just believe that with Jesus you can do it. Say after me; I can win; I can succeed; I can be the best in class; I can be changed; and with God's help I will…
- The greatest asset at man's disposal is faith. You don't need certificates to acquire faith. You don't need human connections to acquire faith. You don't need human approval to acquire faith; you don't need an interview to acquire faith. All you need is your heart, to accept Jesus and to accept His Word.
- The most worthless emotion is self pity. Self-pity destroys beauty; self-pity leads to self disqualification. Self-pity is caused by the devil's lies. Jesus calls you his precious child; He says his love for you will never end. His thoughts for you are thoughts of peace and not of evil and He says your season of miracle is at hand. Cheer up read the Bible and pray today.

> The most beautiful attire is a smile. Refrain from frowning and from anger; put a smile on. Make your world beautiful. Cause your friends to response to your smile by smiling and the world will be a better place to live. Let smiling faces fill our streets; but it takes a smiling heart to get a smiling face. Stop faking smiles, ask Jesus for one today.
> The most prized possession is integrity. It takes a 'man' to walk in integrity. It takes a changed man to maintain integrity. Value integrity and commit yourself to it. Be a man with a godly standard of life. Be a Noah, be a Job and be a Daniel. Be a man of integrity.
> The most powerful channel of communication is prayer. Have you prayed today? Prayer creates your future and develops intimacy with God. A prayer-less man is an empty man. A man of prayer will never lose God's presence and will never be desperate in life.
> The most contagious spirit is enthusiasm. Be zealous for your God given dream and purposes. Don't give any chance for dream killers to destroy your mind with falsehood and human wisdom. Press on and move forward.

Ten prayer request for men and women of purpose
Seek God for:

Health

Pray for constant good health. Stand by faith for your health. For by his stripes you were healed.

Uncommon Provision

Pray for divine provision not just for your needs but for provision for your vision and lifetime dream. Believe God for provision for your projects and for greater establishment.

Protection

pray for God's covenant presence to keep you and all that concerns you safe and protected from the reach of the wicked. I declare Protection of your life, your family, your job, your finances and your investments.

Adequate information

Pray for connection to the information you need for divine placement. Believe for the right information to get to you on time and to move you forward in life.

Divine direction

Pray for the Holy Spirit to direct your life and mind; seek for His guidance and leadership in all your undertakings. It is impossible to fail as long as He leads.

Wise decisions

Pray that no wrong decisions will be taken concerning you; in your work place; in your church or in your community. Pray that the Lord should help you make right decisions in all matters concerning your life and future.

Godly connections

Pray that the Lord should link you up with the right persons for the right results. Pray that God should connect you to the persons that will connect you to your dreamed future and destiny.

Right relationships

Pray that God should help you maintain good relationship with the people that God brings your way. Pray for good relationship with your spouse, your neighbors and with colleagues. Seek not to be an offence to people around you; seek to be a blessing.

Productivity: You were born to be fruitful; pray that God should help you to be fruitful more than your expectation. That your family, community and fellowship will be partakers of your bountiful productiveness in Jesus name.

Fruitfulness

Good management: pray that God should help you manage well all He puts into your hands. Don't be careless; take good care. You were born to reign in life. Give no room for failure and defeats. Take your steps into all that God has for you. Believe and trust God for His covenant Word to be fulfilled in your life. Never give up keep your faith alive. Reign in life with Christ Jesus.

For prayer requests, counseling and to get Bishop Bonnie speak at your event or conference; write to:

World Mission International Worship Center
Email: agborbonnie@gmail.com

Read other books by Dr Bonnie Etta, visit:

www.bishopbonnieettabooks.com

NOTES AND REFERENCES

PART ONE.

CHAPTER ONE

Jos 1/5
Deut 15/6
3 Jn 2.
Deut 1/6-8.
Phi 2/15.
Ps 112/1-3.
Lewis B. Smedes
Gen 50/20-21
2 Sam 13/28
2 Sam 19/10.
Evan ken krivohlavek
Muda Saint Michael
John 4:9
Isa 1:18
Jn 1/10

CHAPTER THREE

7. Deut 7/13-14.
8. Mike Murdock
9. Jn 4/23-24.
10. Rev 4/11.
11. 2Tim 1:7
12. Job 27:5.

13. Pro 14:2.
14. Pr 28:6.
15. Pro 23:7.
16. Ps 119:130.
17. Matt 18:1-5.
18. 2 Cor 5/17

CHAPTER FOUR

1. Josiah Royce
2. Matt 5/9.

CHAPTER FIVE

1. Frederick Keonig
2. By Evan Krivohlaveh Ben.

CHAPTER SIX

1. James Earl Jones.
2. Gen 50:17
3. Gen 42:16.
4. Pro 6:16-19.
5. LK 22:24.
6. John 13:34.
7. John 15:12..
8. John 15:17.
9. Rom 13:8.
10. 1Th 4:9.

CHAPTER SEVEN

1. Ps 119:67.
2. Rom 11:20.
3. Joel 3:14.
4. 1Cor 15:33.

5. Job 36:11.
6. Pr 6:6.
7. Pr 6:9.
8. Pr 10:26.
9. Pr 13:4.
10. Pr 20:4.
11. Pr 26:16.
12. Pr 2:6.
13. Pr 2:7.
14. Pr 2:10.
15. Ps 75:6-7.
16. Exo 14:15.
17. Gen 39:3.
18. Neh 2:20.
19. Gen 24/63-65.
20. Ex 23:25.
21. Mal 4:2.
22. Mt 4:23.
23. Jer 33:6.
24. Ps 107:20.
25. Hos 11:3.
26. 1Co 15:57.
27. 1John 5:4.
28. De 28:7.
29. Rev 3:8.
30. Isa 43:19.
31. Joel 2:25.
32. 1Sa 30:8.
33. Zep 3:18-20.
34. 2Th 3:3.
35. 1Pe 5:10.
36. Rom 16:25-27.
37. Ps 29:11.
38. Ps 37:37.

39. Ps 119:165.
40. Ps 2/1-4

PART TWO

CHAPTER ONE

1. Baruch spinoza
2. 1 Chronicles 4/9-10.
3. Martin Luther king, speech, Aug. 16, 1967
4. Judges 6/ 25-26
5. 1 Kings 11:4-11.
6. 1 Cor 10/ 20.
7. Lev 26/14-32
8. Ex. 20/5-6; Gal 6/6-10
9. 2 Chronicles, 7/14
10. John 1/12.
11. 1 John 1/9
12. Jeremiah, 29/13-14

CHAPTER TWO

1. Eric Hoffer
2. John Calvin
3. Gen 1/28.
4. Genesis 9/1-2
5. Gen 22/15-18.
6. 1 Corinthians 2/10-12.
7. Deuteronomy 2/ 7
8. Deut 15/10.
9. 2 Timothy 1/7.
10. Deut 28/5.
11. Deuteronomy 33/ 13-16.
12. Deut 28/3.
13. Isaiah 57/19.

14. Proverbs 18/20-21.
15. Job 22/28-29.
16. Ezek 37
17. Deuteronomy 7:13-14.
18. Deut 8/18.
19. Gen 22/15-18.

CHAPTER THREE

Arthur Koestler Janus
Saint Augustine
James 5/16
Acts 16/25.
Exo 23/26.
Jer 1/19
Ps 91.
Ps 75/6
9. Luke 10/19-20.
10. Mark 16/9
11. 2 Cor 6/16-18.
12. Mark 5/1-3, 10.
13. Gen 35/1-4.

CHAPTER FOUR

1. Martin Luther King, Jr
2. Rom, 16/20.
3. 1COR15/57
4. Matt 15/13.
5. Jeri 1/10.
6. Gal 4/1-6.
7. 1 Cor 2/12.
8. Oba 17.
9. Deut 1/6-8.
10. 2 Pet 1/3.

11. Deut 1/21.
12. Luke 15/7, 10.
13. 2 Cor 4/3-5.
14. Jeri 62/1-7
15. Joel 2/23-25.
16. Jeri 33/6-7.
17. 1 Sam 30/1-8.
18. Phil 4/19.
19. Ps 2/8.
20. Luke 11/9-13.
21. Mk 11/23.
22. Mk 16/17-18.
23. Matt 16/19.
24. Matt 17/20.
25. Job 22/28.
26. 1Tim 4/14-16.
27. Deut 34/9.
28. Jn 9/7.
29. 2 Kings 5/10.
30. Ex.14/15-16.
31. 2 Sam 1/21.
32. Isa 54/17.
33. Isa 7/7.
34. Ps 23, Ps 27.
35. Ps 91.
36. Eze 37/1-14.
37. Ps 2/1-9.
38. 1 Jn 3/8-9.
39. Isa 7/1-7.
40. Mk 16/17
41. Jer 1/10.
42. Matt 15/13.

CHAPTER FIVE

1. John Maxwell
2. Sven Goran Eriksson quotes
3. 1 Sam 17/50.
4. Judges 15/14-15.
5. Daniel 2/19.
6. Luke 4/18.
7. Isa 10/27.
8. Jud 15/14.
9. Luke 24/49.
10. Acts 1/8.
11. Acts 4/31
12. Zech 4/6.
13. Gen 26/ 12-4.
14. Gen 5/27.
15. 2 kings 10:6.
16. Pro 20/13a.
17. 3 John 1-.
18. Job 36/11-2.
19. 2Cor 4/7-.
20. Jn 16/33.
21. Ralph Cushman

CHAPTER SIX

1. William Blake
2. George Santayana
3. Rom 16/20.

CHAPTER SEVEN

1. Paul J. Meyer
2. Paul J. Meyer quotes

CHAPTER EIGHT

Jackie Windspear
Ralph Waldo Emerson
Acts 4/33-34.
Eph 2:8.
Gen 6:8.
Gen 19:19
Es 2:17.
Est. 5:2
Heb 4:16.
10. Ps 84:11.
11. 1Pe 5:5.
12. Pr 3:34.
13. John 1:16.
14. Ro 5:17.
15. 2Pe 3:18.
16. 2 Pet 1:2.
17. Jude 1:4.
18. Heb 12:28.
19. Jas 4:6.
20. Rom 12: 3.
21. Rom 12:6.
22. Rev 22:21.
23. Zech 12:10.

CHAPTER NINE

1. Stephen S.
2. Japanese Proverb

ABOUT THE AUTHOR

Dr Bonnie Etta is the president of World Mission International School of Ministry. He is the founder and bishop of the World Mission International Worship Center in Maryland, USA. He has been on short-term missionary projects to Germany, Spain, Italy, South Africa, Belgium, and the United Kingdom. He is an international conference speaker and has authored several Christian books. He has yearly church growth conferences in Africa, Europe, and the United States.

Dr Bonnie Etta is happily married to the first lady, Pastor Estella, and are blessed to be the parents of four sons who are very committed to the ministry. He holds a Master Degree in ministry and PhD in theology and philosophy. Bishop Bonnie Etta has been in active ministry for almost three decades. He is worth listening to.

Dr Nojang Evelyn

ABOUT THE BOOK

The book "Living Stress Free" will help you develop Stress Free attitude in order to live Stress Free Life in a stressful world. You will discover and learn how to utilize the seven keys that the author gives the reader to use toward gaining an extraordinary life!

"Stress is a condition that must be dealt with wisely, intelligently and with the help of the Holy Spirit. His presence is true liberty; His fruit is love, joy and peace. His power is the yoke destroyer. Your happiness does not depend on God; it depends on you, and your attitude and response to the daily occurrences of your life."

Living Stress Free is possible.

Dr Bonnie Etta

www.ingramcontent.com/pod-product-compliance
Lightning Source LLC
Chambersburg PA
CBHW071913110526
44591CB00011B/1662